LEGENDS

TOM SHALES

LEGENDS

Remembering America's Greatest Stars

RANDOM HOUSE   NEW YORK

Library of Congress Cataloging-in-Publication Data
Shales, Tom.
Legends / Tom Shales.
p. cm.
ISBN 0-394-57521-0
1. Entertainers—United States.   I. Title.
PN2285.S4   1989
790.2'092'2—dc20   88-43170

Manufactured in the United States of America
Photo research by Diane Cook
9 8 7 6 5 4 3 2
First Edition

Book design by J. K. Lambert

For Kate,

Who remembers

Isn't it romantic?
Merely to be young
On such a night as this.

LORENZ HART
AND RICHARD RODGERS

ACKNOWLEDGMENTS

For their generous help and encouragement, the author thanks James A. Miller, Lee Lawrence, Tom Zito, Howard Simons, Ben Bradlee, Shelby Coffey III, Jeffrey Frank, Andrew Bornstein, Juliette McGrew, Esther Newberg, Brenda A. Caggiano, Amy Roberts, and Peter Osnos.

CONTENTS

INTRODUCTION

Six blocks from the White House on Pennsylvania Avenue stood for years another landmark: the Circle, a small, seedy theater where—before the growing popularity of video cassettes killed off its business, and before wrecking crews leveled it for yet another office building—Washington moviegoers gathered to watch repertory double bills that changed every few days.

At the Circle, I saw King Kong fall for Fay Wray, and Jules and Jim chase Jeanne Moreau, and Fred twirl Ginger around a gazebo, and Charles Foster Kane say his last "Rosebud," and Bing and Bob share a camel to Morocco, and Phyllis Kirk pound Vincent Price's wax face off.

And it was here, at a showing of *Casablanca*, which played the Circle probably dozens of times, that I joined a sizable contingent of the audience who stood up spontaneously one Sunday afternoon and sang along with the crowd of French partisans at Rick's Café Américain. They, and we, were attempting to drown out a German tune sung by Nazi soldiers with our own fervent rendition of "La Marseillaise." We were not rabble, but we were roused. For those of us singing—some who'd learned the lyrics in French class and others who may have learned them from repeated viewings of the film—this was apotheosis vicariosis, a chance almost to step into the movie and thus to live briefly the romantic fantasy we had watched and shared.

At the Circle, popcorn was blah and the floors a bit gummy. The projection could be spotty, and so could the projectionist. One man who took tickets was known to growl. In short, it was not a movie palace. Not until the movie started. Then it became one—a palace of dreams. We were dreamers. We came to see a great picture, we came to see great stars, and we came to partake of legend.

Dictionaries cling to the traditional meaning of legend: a mythic tale handed down from generation to generation. Today the word has, like many superlatives, been devalued, to the point where a twenty-year-old rock star who's had two hit records might be acclaimed as legendary, especially if he makes big messes of his hotel rooms. The world of sports has its own set of rules on this. In the entertainment sphere, where people can now be famous for being famous, they perhaps can also be legends for being legendary. Worse, "notorious" and "infamous" are now widely considered synonyms for "celebrated" and "renowned." Good's bad today, as Cole Porter wrote, and bad's good today, as Michael Jackson keeps saying.

Everything happens more quickly in the age of television, including proclamation of celebrity, coining of household words, and the ascendancies and descendancies of stars. The real legends, once certified, never really descend, though; maybe that's the crucial dividing line. They fit the dictionary definition in that they are mythic and they are handed down from generation to generation. Errol Flynn is now just about as mythic as the Robin Hood he played in the movies. Indeed, Warner Brothers studios, where he made the film in 1938, may have achieved a mythic status well beyond that of Sherwood Forest. MGM was a land of Oz, Columbia a Shangri-la, RKO a Xanadu. Tiny Republic was the vast, wild West.

True legends are larger than life, and yet usually dead. James Dean became a legend because he died so young, but mostly, the legends in popular culture are those who compiled admirable, perhaps astonishing, bodies of work over long and productive lives. There had to be, of course, something more—more than excellence, more than brilliance (excellence and brilliance might not even be that important to it), an indefinable peculiarity that, one trusts, will never be successfully synthesized in a test tube nor reduced to a breakdown of chemical components. We may eventually understand genius. But legend, no.

It's an eye-of-the-beholder kind of thing, and neither the eyes nor the beholders can be put under a microscope or through a computer, not that marketing whizzes and audience-measurement experts don't keep trying.

If legends didn't tend to be dead, then the phrase "living legend" would not have been invented. People are spoken of as legends in their own time or, less charitably, as legends in their own mind. So-and-so has "become a legend," TV newscasters and sportscasters say. And a famous mink coat company asked in a long series of magazine ads, "What becomes a legend most?" All of those shown wearing the mink coats were indeed alive at the time the ads ran. Were they really legends yet? It's a gray area, and kind of a purple area, too, but probably not.

Obviously allowances have to be made. Frank Sinatra seems

to have been the stuff of legend almost from Day One—or Day Two, anyway. Bette Davis became a legend about the time, ironically or not, that her career lay in ruins. She was alive and legendary nevertheless, and eventually her popularity swelled again. Joan Crawford, on the other hand, had to die; nothing short of that would suffice. Davis, asked by reporters for comment shortly after Crawford's demise, is supposed to have said, "A person doesn't change just because they're dead." Maybe persons themselves don't, but perceptions do. Persons die, and legends are born.

"Living legend" is like "living saint"; it implies an exception to a rule. Well-balanced people do not literally worship legends of the screen—movie or television—but these figures do take on resemblances to religious icons. The Circle Theater was a temple, maybe a house of worship, and some of us had quasi-religious experiences there.

Once, the Circle Theater was playing compilations of comedy shorts from the silent years of cinema. I sat behind a father who'd brought his little boy, seven or eight years old, as a way of introducing him to classic comedy. The kid had never seen Charlie Chaplin. Each time a new silent clown appeared on the screen, he would ask his father if that one was Chaplin. No, that was Harry Langdon. No, that was Buster Keaton. No, that was Harold Lloyd.

The boy and his dad sat through the parade of comics, the kid not reacting much to their comedy. And then the Little Tramp in the inflated pants and jaunty bowler came on the screen. Yes, the father told the son, that was Charlie Chaplin. At this cue, the kid began to laugh uproariously. Ah, Charlie Chaplin—one laughs. The little boy's was the loudest laughter in the house. He was laughing at a shabby man getting the best of rich people and cops and doing flip-flops and pratfalls, and he was paying his own homage to a legend, even if he didn't realize it.

Charlie Chaplin was still alive then, living in Switzerland. Maybe he heard that laughter. Maybe he hears it now.

No people who lived on this planet in any previous century ever had the opportunity to link up with images of the dear departed as lifelike as those available to us now on film and tape. It's still an eerie, relatively new challenge to consciousness, a way of almost, almost cheating mortality. Such images are going to get more and more lifelike as technology progresses, assuming it does progress. How will it affect us when we can beam three-dimensional holograms of Gary Cooper or the late Aunt Milly into our living rooms? Our rooms of the living dead?

Death still has its sting, all right, and all the last laughs, but our concept of it is altered by media. In a piquant movie called *Hot Tomorrows* that Martin Brest directed while still a film student, the hero turns on a TV set and watches the zany antics of Laurel and Hardy with morbid fascination rather than amusement. "I love television," he says. "It lets you enter the land of the dead."

Being dead is not what it used to be. It can even seem a zany antic itself. For some celebrities, death is not even necessarily an impediment to earning power. The Elvis Presley estate reportedly grossed $15 million in 1988 through licensing deals and tours of Presley's Graceland mansion. For much of that year, Presley turned up on the cover of at least one supermarket tabloid a week: A statue of Elvis had been found on Mars; a picture of Elvis had wept real tears; though dead, it seems Elvis still fathered children.

No wonder legends are sometimes called immortals.

Other stars have made posthumous fortunes, or at least tidy incomes. Abbott and Costello, the buoyant comedy team of the forties and fifties, took in about half a million dollars in 1988 through licensing fees of their likenesses, according to *Forbes* magazine; two actors imitating them sold a bran cereal, for one thing. More people have seen Abbott and Costello movies since their deaths than saw them while they were alive. Each man died virtually insolvent.

Chaplin's Little Fellow, who had valiantly rebelled against encroaching technocracy in *Modern Times*, was licensed by IBM and became a mascot for computers. A child who saw a Charlie Chaplin movie now would say, "Oh, there's the little man from the commercials." Everything has its price, even legendariness.

It would be comforting to think that people will continue to distinguish between likenesses and genuine articles, except that what have we left of Marilyn Monroe, really, but a ghost on strips of celluloid, or a magnetic imprint on tape, or photographs on a page? She's there, but not really there; she is with us, but gone. At least film and tape have made it possible for succeeding generations to perceive what it was that made the legends legendary—why, in a world where everyone is allegedly "special," some were extraspecial, of a specialness unique and totally distinctive.

One has to take it on faith, really, that Eleonora Duse and Sarah Bernhardt were hot stuff. Only primitive recordings or films of them remain. But nobody should ever have to wonder what made Fred Astaire great, or why Ingrid Bergman knocked people for a loop, or how Cary Grant managed to charm the pants off everybody in the place. It's as plain as the nose on Jimmy Durante's face.

From the preserved recorded work of luminaries this luminous, we get more than entertainment and diversion now. We get sustenance, affirmation, enrichment, even exaltation: yes, somebody was that good, people can be that good, he or she was everything he or she was cracked up to be. Legends can hold up even when their vehicles explode under them: The Marx Brothers might have been chastized for a dud like *Love Happy* in its time, but today it is part of the festival. Even legends are entitled to a bad day. A bad week. A bad year.

Once you're in, though, you're here to stay.

The object all-sublime is when both the performer and the performed combine to reach some perfect, rarefied pinnacle of lunatic beauty, like John Barrymore and Carole Lombard in *Twentieth Century* or Humphrey Bogart and Katharine Hepburn in *The African Queen*, or you-name-him and you-name-her in You-Name-It. *Casablanca* isn't really a movie anymore. It's a commingling of memories, illusions, allusions, and, perhaps, delusions.

"Nostalgia" doesn't quite cover it, though there is in the work of past masters the abiding solace of escape from the present. It's always the present, never the past or the future, from which one seeks escape. Even if the future looks bleak, at least it'll be a change in the status quo. Until President Kennedy was killed, it was possible to have nostalgia for the present; to wish it would go on forever just this way, and not to care very much for looking backward. Since that time, the past has grown lucratively marketable. Now, it is constantly replayed and recycled through television, and though this led me to call the eighties the Re Decade, it's likely the nineties will be mostly reruns, too.

Browsing through cable TV is like sifting through old boxes in the attic. You turn the channel and you never quite know what year you'll find yourself in. As life and death have become relative in the media age, so have "then" and "now." Perhaps it's true that the past has become more attractive in direct proportion to the decline of faith in the future. Or perhaps it's just that the old days, particularly the good ones, have never been so accessible.

We're perhaps never again going to feel as well off as we imagine we once were. People even become nostalgic for World War II or the Depression because of the bold moral choices they presented and the stark contrasts between good and evil, right and wrong. Shirley Temple's dancing with Bill Robinson brings back certain reassurances; lost innocence is found innocence.

I have to confess that feelings of nostalgia come easily to me, and always have. At six, I'm sure I was nostalgic for five. I can still remember the pangs of longing I suffered when I had to leave elementary school behind for the new frontier of junior high. I did not boldly go. But as long as it's kept within reason, I don't see anything wrong with looking back fondly on happy times, or even with exaggerating how happy they were.

We remember happy times because most of us really didn't realize how happy they were when we were living through them.

Today it is commonly lamented that today's stars and superstars will make poor excuses for legends tomorrow—a legend gap looms. Who will there be to accept the entertainment "life achievement" awards twenty or thirty years from now? The bestowers of such prizes are running out of names already. Will middle-aged ex-yuppies of 2001 work themselves into weepy lathers looking back on golden days of Rob Lowe and Michelle Pfeiffer, Bangles and Bon Jovi, Michael J. Fox and Vanna White? Or even Bruce Springsteen, adored now as if he were a god?

The stars considered true legends now didn't consider themselves legends at the time, and they didn't seem to be worried much about posterity. Fred Astaire called himself a hoofer and said that when he made his musicals with Ginger Rogers and others, it was simply a matter of earning a living. Bing Crosby said he was worried about making a buck and never thought of himself as particularly splendid at singing or acting. These performers didn't ever, so far as I can tell, talk publicly their "needs as an artist" the way the grubbiest, goofiest rock star does now.

No matter how essentially celebratory the experience of revisiting old films and television shows and recordings may be, there's always the element of sadness there, too. If you look through the family scrapbook and come upon a photo of grandpa with a parakeet on his head, you may laugh, but then you also feel a tinge of lamentation: Grandpa is gone and the parakeet with him. Television is the national scrapbook now—where movies and programming and news events and fashions are perpetually recycled—and one browses through it with mixed emotions.

Even old programs that are watched mainly for their quaint boringness, like *Leave It to Beaver* or the deliriously uneventful *Adventures of Ozzie and Harriet*, can make one a little misty and melancholy. You catch Ozzie clearing up a frivolous misunderstanding about a night out with the boys and you think, Imagine. This is all it once took to keep people entertained. Well maybe not entertained, but moderately diverted. Placated. Mollified. Sedated? Drugged into submission? Whatever—it worked, and in some strange way it can still work, if on another level, particularly as refuge from prevailing aggressive cacophony.

Ozzie, we hardly knew ye. And that's the way we liked it. Stars of yesteryear were, of course, far less accessible than most of today's, who always seem ready and willing to share innermost thoughts and marital data and open the doors of their homes to peripatetic snoops. Fan magazines of the past weren't the same as this kind of celebrity voyeurism; mainly they created fictional stars whom audiences had seen playing fictional characters on the screen. There was a gentlepersons' agreement; the really lurid gossip wasn't printed. You just got on the horn and blabbed it all over town.

Perhaps this is one reason it will be harder for stars of today to become legends of tomorrow. We know so damn much about them, more than we may know about the next-door neighbors. And, of course, television breeds and exploits chummy intimacy, whereas the movies, oversized and sprayed on a wall above us, were a land of distant giants.

In a Warner Brothers wartime revue called *Thank Your Lucky Stars,* an actress playing a woman in the audience at a stage show looks at the program to see who's next on the bill and exclaims to her husband in the next seat, "Oh, look, Bette Davis! She's my favorite star!" Movie audiences watching that at the time may have themselves hooted at the slack-jawed gushiness, but it suggests the way stars were regarded in another day, which is not the way they are regarded now.

Contemplating stars of other eras, one sees stardom as it used to be, and what it used to mean. It used to mean, in a word, more, partly because people were probably more open to being wowed; partly because there was less cynicism in the world; partly because stars didn't whine a lot in public about pressures and demands put upon them. Gazing at stars of then and now tells us something about the times, the zeitgeist, the grim and frivolous realities. The way they were does correlate with the way we were or would have been. And if they look good, we imagine we did, too. People cannot be blamed for preferring rosy backward glances to hard, cold close-ups from a mirror.

Not a year goes by that some new young actor isn't hailed by some observer of the scene as the new Cary Grant. There've been a number of new Clark Gables, too. But they never are Cary Grant, and they never are Clark Gable. There was a first generation of Hollywood legends, and they are going to remain the standard by which all others are judged. First impressions, in this case, reign. If stars of today seem pale and one-dimensional compared to those of another time, however, the blessing of hindsight may eventually even things out. The fault may lie not in our stars but in ourselves.

In the artifice of other times, there's something real to which one can connect, and it may come across as more "real" than the artifice of today does. Movie stars of the thirties and forties were pressed, powdered, pampered, and plopped before us (and, most of them, kept on very short tethers by their bosses); the best craftsmanship enhanced and supported them. Even so, if there hadn't been something extraordinary there in the first place, the fluff and filigree wouldn't have worked. It would have been like trying to turn a wan gray lump of a politician into a telegenic cutie-pie. The raw materials have to exist in some measure, or the transparency will be blinding.

Stars are elected, in a way; the public does choose them. At first, movie producers didn't want stars to be stars, didn't even want them identified by name. But the audience began referring to a certain sweet young thing forever overcoming adversities on the screen as "Mary," and so Mary Pickford was christened and born. No matter how elaborate the trappings, from Busby Berkeley's kaleidoscopic chorines to the laser blasts and vaporized planets of *Star Wars* and its progeny, it's still people that people come to see.

I never dreamed the past would be so long ago. Years that only yesterday seemed like yesterday are now faded and remote. When people tell me I graduated from college more than twenty years ago, I can't believe them, any more than when they tell me that John F. Kennedy has been dead for more than a quarter-century, or that *The Wizard of Oz* has celebrated its fiftieth birthday, or that there are young parents today who not only never knew life without television, but who never knew life without color television.

Soon there will be parents who never knew life without a VCR.

Claude Rains as Major Renault scoffs that Bogart as Rick Blaine has turned out to be a "sentimentalist" after all. Sentimentalists have always been derided. But if it was good enough for Monsieur Rick, it's good enough for me. I despair when stars die, especially those who could be put in the category of legends.

Most of the pieces in this book were written within hours after the deaths of the personalities profiled, and they were meant not as obituaries, but as appreciations, a term given them at *The Washington Post* about the time I did my first one, an ode to Bing Crosby written on the day he died. I remember getting the news of Crosby's death in the office and feeling terribly emptied by it. Sometime later, sitting in the same office, I heard of the death of a beautiful and much-loved coworker. The sense of loss was more intense, yet not dissimilar.

Does every star's death diminish me? Let's not overdo it. But in the past decade or two, many of the venerable, established entertainers I saw on television of the fifties and sixties, and onstage, and in movies at the Circle Theater and elsewhere, have reached the end of their roads, and it's been hard to watch as this particular performing generation expires. These people seemed troupers and pros and dynamos, and also had, again, that mercurial something that set them apart, made them seemed destined for greatness of some sort. They were members of an extended family, photos in an album, friends one almost knew.

I never met Bing Crosby, but many of those I profiled, and appreciated, I had interviewed—or at least encountered in person—somewhere along the way. The first time I met Cary Grant, I was covering a White House social occasion. Reporters had to wait outside the closed doors of the State Dining Room for the guests to emerge. The one I most wanted to meet was

Grant, though the president was in there, and probably a potentate or two, and members of the capital glitterati, such as it glitters.

But to meet Cary Grant! Now you're talking. The doors of the dining room opened and Cary Grant was the first one out. He seemed to burst forth. I marched up and said something, who knows what, and he smiled and was gracious and congenial. Starstruck I was not; there weren't many stars whom it would have given me that much of a kick to meet. And sometimes when you did meet them, they were disappointing—rude or aloof or vaguely senile. Cary Grant acted precisely the way you would want Cary Grant to act. To the manners born.

My time with Fred Astaire was brief, to say the most. All night long at a New York gala, I'd been promised a few moments with him by perspiring publicists. I got those few moments: an elevator ride from the sixty-fifth-floor Rainbow Room of the RCA Building to the lobby. Gene Kelly was on the elevator, too, leading me to speculate that if it crashed and we all died, my name would not make the newspaper accounts. Astaire was indeed shy, and self-effacing; that was evident even in those fleeting minutes. He was blissfully unpretentious.

When the elevator reached the ground floor and the doors opened, Gene Kelly bowed grandly and said, "After you, Mr. Astaire." That seemed the proper gesture of deference, even if he had done it facetiously.

Ingrid Bergman was tense and a little persnickety, and dragged heavily on cigarettes, but when she smiled, her eyes moist, that old feeling came back. Rosalind Russell was precisely the tough, wisecracking buzz bomb she'd been in so many hard-boiled comedies. Natalie Wood had deep, dark, sexy eyes and an intoxicating, inviting smile, but she also had a sardonic sense of humor about Hollywood and its absurdities.

Television may be a medium of scaling down, but some of those who've flowered there have been larger than life, too. Dave Garroway had an intense curiosity that was mesmerizing; he was wildly interested in the world. Jackie Gleason was a dandy—a dan-dan-dandy, as he used to say—and a sport, rakishly elegant. I never met Burr Tillstrom, and he came out from behind his Kuklapolitan proscenium only for a quick bow at the end of his TV show, but after my review of one of his specials was published in 1973, he sent me a letter in which he said, "To be understood and appreciated is all that one can ask—and it's all the world to a creative thinker." At the bottom, near his signature, he drew his two most famous characters and under them wrote, "Kukla and Ollie, too."

Hanging out at NBC when the original *Saturday Night Live* was riding high, I ran into John Belushi several times. Sometimes he would just blast past, yelling and worrying, minutes before airtime. Whenever there was a chance to talk, he was boyish and ingratiating. He and other core members of the troupe came to Washington early in the run of the show and cavorted their way from monument to monument, joking and clowning not for me, or any other audience, but for each other.

With Belushi, the playful irreverence seemed genuine and endemic. And though at the other end of the comic spectrum, Jack Benny was boyish and playful, too, still sort of wide-eyed at eighty and given to extravagant gestures and rapt hyperbole, much as he was when in character on radio and TV. Alfred Hitchcock tried to remain in character, the morbid prankster he played in all his publicity, but you knew you were in the company of a master. Lucille Ball seemed distracted and remote through much of the interview, but then at the end she smiled warmly and graciously, years of star training having done their job.

Are all these people legends? Maybe not to everybody, but for members of certain generations, they are. Or should be. The list here is anything but all-inclusive, even for the decade and a half of star departures it encompasses. A few writers, producers, and directors of especially high profile are included along with performers. Some conspicuously absent stars are missing because there doesn't seem to be one more word that can be said about them—unless, that is, it should be a debunking word. The profiles in this collection are not of the warts-and-all variety. You have to find the warts elsewhere. These are people who earned the right to be remembered for what they did well. It really doesn't matter, for these purposes, if they were beastly to their children.

Of course, the approach is shamelessly subjective and, more than that, has a built-in bias, that not only of a television critic, but of a TV-raised child, a teleboomer. I got my first exposure to many of these legends (and to much of life, for good or ill) through the tube—impressions both of those whom television gave great fame and glory, and those already renowned from other fields. I can remember a time when television was more amazing than appalling. It was quite a few years ago.

What all the legends in this book have in common, the thread that binds, is that every one of them was one of a kind. You wouldn't confuse them with anybody else. They made marks even in heavily marked times; they stood out among standouts. Kleenex culture ours now may be—fast-frozen, disposable, microwavable. But some things last. They are worth noting.

When the big stars die, they get a last curtain call on the networks' evening newscasts. Obits, most of them prepared in advance, combine quick clips of greatest hits, the stars in happy firmament. What comes after the final bow? Time flies when you're dead. Blitzed by media and their perpetual shower of hot new names, we may be guilty of neglecting the old ones. Then a certain movie will play the late show, or somebody mounts a tribute, and the impressions are fresh again, back to trigger myriad personal associations of Where We Were When.

Sometimes an old movie or TV show makes me think audiences of the past were ingrates. *It's a Wonderful Life* was a flop in its original release; *Citizen Kane* didn't do all that well. What was the matter with people? Didn't they know what they had? They took for granted some movies that are considered epochal classics now, and stars of incomparable incandescence. The perspective of time is a great clarifier, and yet a great romanticizer, too.

Once, at the Circle Theater, I sat through a double bill of *42nd Street* and *Dames,* two Depression-era musicals, and then sat through both of them again. Not that they were such terrific movies; but this was in pre-VCR days, and who knew when they would be around again? Better just to enjoy the hell out of them while the opportunity presented itself. Old movies are not messages in a bottle but messages in a can; your consciousness may not always be raised, but it's bound to be jostled a little.

How green was my valley the first time I saw *How Green Was My Valley.* And the fourth or fifth time, too.

The original Circle is long gone, to be replaced by one of those omni-multi-mega-plex jobs. Perhaps the floors won't be gummy or the popcorn blah, and all the ticket-takers cheery sprites. A computer will run the projectors, probably with great efficiency. But nothing could improve on the Circle as it exists in memory. Memory is the greatest museum of all, and you can carry it around with you. It doesn't hurt to dust off the exhibits now and again. I sat down with a bottle of beer one afternoon and watched *Casablanca* on TV again, for either the umpteenth or the nth time, and remembering along with the movie seemed to make me remember everything about everything. It became a celebration of remembering—remembering, and attempting to recapture.

If humans are the only animals that blush or need to, they're also the only animals that get nostalgic or want to. It's something that sets us apart from the lower orders, just as regretting and complaining do. Dogs and cats and apes are denied the ineffable comforts that self-indulgent sentimentality can bring.

I really did have an Aunt Milly, by the way, though I am sure I will never see her in a hologram. There is a single sharp, specific memory of her, however, that is virtually holographic. We were in a bakery—my mother, Aunt Milly, and me—and Mother was ordering something from behind the counter. Aunt Milly was looking at a record album I'd just bought. I told her I knew all the songs but one, and pointed to the title. She said it was an old favorite of hers, and leaning down, sang it to me aloud, right there in the middle of the crowded shop. It was "Something to Remember You By," which begins, "Oh give me something to remember you by, when I am far away from you. . . ."

She is far away from me now. But she gave me that, and it will always be close.

LEGENDS

B ing Crosby's reign outlasted all the heirs apparent. They came, they went, they did or did not acknowledge the debt they owed him, he stayed. Even when Crosby's record sales grew insignificant and rock took over for good, it was encouraging to know that Crosby was still there—still there, happily hanging around like some venerated ex-president. A chief executive. He was not your everyday superstar.

You realized how much his music meant to you, and the innumerable connections it could make, when you heard Crosby's soothing croon coming from a gaudy jukebox in a two-bit bar on that lonely holiday away from home. You heard Bing singing "White Christmas" and you were home again. A thousand memories welled up. You could warm your hands on the sound of his voice.

If he inspired the occasional sentimental binge, Crosby didn't sentimentalize himself. Just the opposite. He was the very absence of pretentiousness, even when it was estimated that his voice had been heard by more people than that of any other mortal who ever lived. Through it all, Bing was jaunty and blithe and self-effacing. He did it in a stroll. It was a particularly American way of dealing with fame and glory; he made it look disarmingly attractive.

"All I do is, I just do the same old thing every time," Bing told an interviewer in 1975, "except each time, it's a different song." And in a way, each time it was the same song, too.

A year later, he tried analyzing his style for the London *Times*. "I wanted to sing conversationally, to reach people with the meaning," he said. "I don't think of a song in terms of notes. I try to think of what it purports to say lyrically. That way it sounds more natural, and anything natural is more listenable."

People forget that this master of the middle of the road led a revolution in popular music, away from oratory and into conversation. Singers were coming into the house on the radio; they no longer needed to pontificate and declaim to throngs. Bing was one of the first singers to sing just to you, wherever you were; his songs were as personal as a phone call from a friend. It was not a high-blown, artsy approach, yet Crosby helped make popular song one of the true art forms of the century.

And he found time to conquer other worlds. He scored a genuine dramatic triumph in the movie version of the Clifford Odets play *The Country Girl*, playing a broken-down alcoholic singing actor named Frank Elgin. More than in his popular priest movies—*The Bells of St. Mary's* and *Going My Way*—Crosby showed in this one he could really act. In key stages of Frank Elgin's boozy deterioration, Crosby must have called upon his own early bouts with the bottle; it made the portrayal convincing and stark.

Still, that *was* Bing Crosby up there. In the film, playgoers at intermission discuss the musical and its star as they stand outside the theater. A woman is telling her husband, "I'm sure you've seen him before—years ago in that show that took place in Central Park."

"Oh, is he the same one?" the husband asks.

"So easygoing and likable, isn't he?" she says.

When it comes to Crosby movies, though, it's more cheering to remember him romping around with Bob Hope in the madcap *Road* pictures they made together. Hope said once that the atmosphere on the set was so festive that "guys used to fight to get to work on the pictures." Then he sighed and said, "God, it was fun."

Theirs was a public, show-biz friendship that remained entertaining on radio, television, and even in newsreels, as well as in the *Road* movies, where the jokes were often at Crosby's expense. In one of the films, Hope suddenly hears violins sneaking in on the soundtrack. He looks into the camera and says, "Okay, folks, you can go out for popcorn now; he's going to sing again."

Crosby popped up in cameos in many of Hope's other comedies. At the end of *My Favorite Brunette*, Crosby plays the executioner on duty the day Hope's execution is called off. He is referred to by his real first name, "Harry." When he stomps away, disappointed he doesn't get to throw the switch, Hope confides to the camera, "He'll take any kind of a part."

At the beginning of Hope's western *Son of Paleface*, Crosby appears on the screen driving a car. In narration, Hope explains that Crosby is "an old character actor" on the Paramount lot who is given small roles out of charity. The *Road* pictures would stop in their tracks for Hope and Crosby to swap insults or extend their radio feud. "You've got that something in your voice so right for selling cheese," Hope sang, a reference to

Crosby's radio sponsor, Kraft. Crosby sang back, "I think your jokes are funny; it's just that folks are hard to please."

This wasn't just comedy; it was merriment.

One respected Crosby in particular for the things about his life that he kept private. Though he played a priest several times, his Catholicism remained something personal; he didn't drag God into his act, and when he sang religious numbers, it was without schmaltz. Not even Barbara Walters could seriously penetrate the Crosby wall of privacy.

In the last decade of his life, after a long period of virtual retirement, Crosby softly stepped back into the spotlight, and millions of people were reminded how much they loved him. Sometimes he turned up in unlikely places. When one of his pet topics, tequila, was discussed in the pages of the rock mag *Rolling Stone,* Crosby wrote a friendly letter to the editor disputing a few points about the pungent delicacy. The letter was published and followed with an editor's note assuring readers that yes, this was the real Bing Crosby.

And when, during a celebration of his fifty years in show business, Crosby took an unfortunate tumble from a tricky stage in Pasadena, and photographers rushed forward and stood on the stage looking down at him and were asked not to take any pictures as Crosby lay there injured, they complied. They recognized him as the cultural equivalent of a head of state.

Crosby's career was dissected in, of all forums, *The Village Voice,* where writer Gary Giddens, after scolding Crosby somewhat for forsaking pure jazz to do homogenized pop, suggested Crosby had come to play the role not only of troubador but of ombudsman. "He reminds me of a line in an old Carl Reiner–Mel Brooks routine about a pop singer who says of his audience, 'I am them, they are me, we are all singing, I have the mouth,' " Giddens wrote.

Calling Crosby "the ultimate pop icon," Giddens said, "He is us, and we are him, only he has the mouth."

There will probably never be another singer as widely, universally popular as Bing Crosby. Part of the fallout of the media explosion is a fractionalized electorate; the great audience has become many audiences. Radio stations play all this and all that, all day. Where Crosby's influence will end we can never know, however. No matter what kind of music a singer performs, whenever there's an attempt to make individual, personal communication in song, Bing Crosby's legacy is perpetuated.

He titled his autobiography *Call Me Lucky,* and every indication is, that's how he really thought of himself.

Bing sang so many songs it would be hard to find a common thread through them, but some of those most associated with him had a Crosbyesque message: Relax, take it easy, don't worry, be happy.

He sang Irving Berlin's "Lazy" in *Holiday Inn.* He sang "Gone Fishin' " with Louis Armstrong, "Don't Fence Me In" with the Andrew Sisters, and "In the Cool, Cool, Cool of the Evening" with Jane Wyman. He sang of "The Land of Beginning Again" and he sang the musical advice "Accentuate the Positive" and "Count Your Blessings (Instead of Sheep)." He sang American credos and gave them new credibility.

It was a voice of comfort, a voice of cheer. It was even a voice of reason. It was a voice to come home to. It was a voice as big as all indoors.

~~~~~~~~~~~~~~~~~~~~~~~~~~~~~~~~~~~~~~~
~~~~~~~~~~~~~~~~~~~~~~~~~~~~~~~~~~~~~~~
~~~~~~~~~~~~~~~~~~~~~~~~~~~~~~~~~~~~~~~

To have walked on the moon, that would be nice. But to dance like Fred Astaire—that would be heaven. Grace does not come naturally to humans, but it appeared to come naturally to him. Often, on the movie screen, Fed Astaire had seemed better than mortal; he improved on perfection. He defied the laws of nature so regularly in films that one hoped he could defy them in real life—that he would live, and dance, forever.

Fred Astaire danced up the walls and across the ceiling in *Royal Wedding*; he danced on rooftops and ledges and the Washington Square arch in *The Belle of New York*; he danced on roller skates in *Shall We Dance?*; and he danced with fire-crackers popping at his heels in *Holiday Inn*.

He danced where angels feared to tread. He had shoes with wings on.

Nobody danced as well as Fred Astaire; this was an absolute, a given, a certainty. And nobody looked quite so comfortable dancing, either. The man was at home on his feet. He relaxed in motion. There was more to it than agility and finesse; it was a total package deal. Fred Astaire was born to the dance as some are born to the priesthood. It called, and he heard it.

Most memorably, Fred Astaire danced with Ginger Rogers in a series of thirties romantic musicals best represented perhaps by *Top Hat.* That was the film in which Ginger complained about Fred's tap dancing in the hotel suite above hers and, as an apology, he spilled sand on the floor and soft-shoed her to sleep. Later they twirled each other around a gazebo in the park after Fred had popped the musical question, "Isn't this a lovely day to be caught in the rain?"

In private, associates have said, Fred was not fond of Ginger and detested her overbearing mother. But together on the screen they were, as Arlene Croce wrote (quoting a lyric from *Swing Time*), "*La belle, la* perfectly swell romance." A fine romance, with no kisses—or hardly any. They didn't have to kiss when they could dance like that. This was the most rarefied form of communication ever invented. Who could watch without wanting to be one of them?

They did the Continental, they did the Carioca, they did the Piccolino and the Yam, and in *The Gay Divorcee,* he crooned "Night and Day" into her ear. Astaire sang quite well, and composers loved him because he didn't mess around with the lyrics. He introduced songs by the Gershwins, Cole Porter, and Irving Berlin, and in time came to epitomize the age in which such men wrote such songs. Fred Astaire represented effortless elegance, never studied, and he wore top hat and tails as few men could.

On his Emmy-winning TV specials in the 1960s, Astaire donned the formal outfit again, telling the audience on one occasion that he used to hate to wear tails "but now that I've got them on again . . . I *loathe* them." One associates him with a time of grace and glamour and manners, but Astaire also personified a classy, uncomplaining professionalism.

To make it look easy and natural, Astaire spent weeks in rehearsal on his dance numbers, and he insisted that directors shoot him so his whole body could be seen in the frame. There wasn't to be any cheating. They didn't have to fix it in the editing because it was already fixed in rehearsal.

When it all fell into place, it fell just right. Everyone has a personal favorite Astaire moment. For many it's the piquant "Never Gonna Dance" number from *Swing Time,* for others the brooding "Let's Face the Music and Dance" from *Follow the Fleet.* In the otherwise undistinguished *The Sky's the Limit,* Astaire danced the dramatic monologue "One for My Baby," which ends with his smashing the glassware and mirrors behind a bar in angry desperation. "You'd never know it," he sang to the bartender, "but buddy, I'm a kind of poet, and I've got a lot of things to say."

But you would know it. He was a kind of poet. His range went far beyond suave sophistication, to such priceless encounters as the "Couple of Swells" bum number with Judy Garland in *Easter Parade* and a comic romp through an amusement park, "Stiff Upper Lip," with George Burns and Gracie Allen in *A Damsel in Distress.*

There were many partners besides Rogers: Rita Hayworth, Cyd Charisse, Audrey Hepburn, Leslie Caron, Jane Powell, Joan Fontaine, and, on television, Barrie Chase. In *The Band Wagon,* he danced a duet with British music-hall star Jack Buchanan, "I Guess I'll Have to Change My Plan," which always quietly manages to bring the house down. In *Royal Wedding,* he danced with a hat rack and in *Easter Parade* with a fleet of shoes and ballet slippers.

In *Blue Skies,* he danced with multiple images of himself, but even a platoon of special-effects Astaires couldn't upstage Fred Astaire. There was still, always would be, always will be, only one. Some people have style. He *was* style.

Dramatic roles, in later years, kept him occupied. His was a career of nearly unstoppable longevity. He appeared in a TV movie with Helen Hayes and played such other straight dramatic parts as a suicidal scientist in *On the Beach.* Even if he didn't dance, the way he walked or jingled the change in his pocket or even turned his head still seemed dancer's movements. One wondered if he was capable of tripping over a rumpled rug, or hitting his thumb with a hammer. He seemed in complete harmony with the universe. He improved on perfection.

In the compilation film *That's Entertainment,* as preface to a clip from *Broadway Melody of 1940* in which Astaire danced with Eleanor Powell, narrator Frank Sinatra said, "You know, you can wait around and hope, but you'll never see the likes of this again." Together, Fred and Eleanor snapped and crackled across a shiny dance floor while Artie Shaw and the band played "Begin the Beguine." Maybe, indeed, it never got better than that. Maybe it's been all downhill from there.

In *Top Hat*, Fred cooes to Ginger, "Oh I love to climb a mountain, and to reach the highest peak, but it doesn't thrill me half as much as dancing cheek to cheek." In the movies since, we have seen armies march, nations fall, and worlds collide. Monsters have arrived from other planets and risen up from the deep. Passions have flared and seas parted and kingdoms crumbled.

But it hasn't thrilled us half as much as watching Fred Astaire.

~~~
~~~
~~~

ackie Gleason breezed into Washington one warm May day, and here was a guy who knew how to breeze. He planned to meet his wife, Marilyn, and take the Concorde to Paris. Supersonic travel was still fairly new then, and Gleason was asked if he had ever gone faster than the speed of sound before. He said, "Only a couple of times at Toots Shor's."

He was sitting at a French provincial desk in the penthouse suite of a luxury hotel. The waiter stopped pouring the Beaujolais a tad too soon, and Gleason signaled him to continue. "Go all the way," he said. He was ensconced and he was resplendent. There was a trademark red carnation in his lapel, and well into his sixties, he still came across as a confident, dapper rascal.

But the Concorde sounded out of character. Gleason reportedly had a steadfast aversion to air travel. "Well, that's a legend, pal," Gleason said, "and you don't fight the legends. If people want to say I don't fly, that's okay with me."

Of all the bulls who roared and romped through the china shop of television, Gleason cut the widest swath. That had nothing to do with his celebrated girth (you didn't fight that legend, either) but with his dauntless range and tenacity. He was often known to overdo; he was never known to overreach.

It was Orson Welles, Gleason said, who nicknamed him the Great One, during one of their nightclubbing jags in the fifties. It fit. As Welles had found his toy train set in a Hollywood movie studio a decade earlier, Gleason found his in television land. CBS was a playground for him; he was given money instead of candy. As a notable acquisition of CBS founder-chairman William S. Paley, Gleason joined an incomparably stellar stable. It's unlikely we'll ever see such a collection of talent in one place again.

But then, you could look at Gleason and say it is unlikely we'll ever see such a collection of talent in one man again.

On his network variety show, Gleason was an entire rogues' gallery. Of all the characters he played week in and week out, the one with the greatest durability and most pungency has been, of course, Ralph Kramden, the long-suffering and pipe-dreaming Madison Avenue bus driver, who lived in a dingy Brooklyn tenement with his flinty wife, Alice, and who regularly bowled and verbally brawled with his best friend, sewer worker Ed Norton. *The Honeymooners* was television's first true blue-collar opera, a kitchen-sink comedy to rival the kitchen-sink dramas of the live TV fifties. Gleason's portly proletarian Ralph was spiritual kin to Paddy Chayefsky's embittered butcher Marty.

As a fictional creation very much of his time, Ralph Kramden can stand proudly beside such literary brothers of the era as Arthur Miller's Willy Loman and Tennessee Williams's Stanley Kowalski. Really.

RALPH: "I'm big news, Alice! I'm a hero! A hero! A heee-RO! You know what a hero is?"

ALICE: "Yeah. It's a fat sandwich that's full of baloney."

There is a tragic as well as a comic stature to Ralph and his aspirations to upward mobility, all of them thrashed or thwarted. The bleakness of the Kramden surroundings (the apartment set photographed like a slum interior from an old D. W. Griffith melodrama), the aching childlessness of Ralph and Alice (dealt with directly in only one or two installments), and the unbridled bravado with which Ralph heralds the arrival of each new cock-eyed scheme, all combine to keep *The Honeymooners* dimensional and valid. The grubby details come from Gleason's own impoverished youth. "Everybody knew a guy like Ralph Kramden," he said once, "and there were a million Ed Nortons."

It wasn't a documentary, though, it was theater, and the portrayals of Ralph and Alice by Gleason and Audrey Meadows (others played the role, none as well), and by Art Carney as Norton, are now so iconographic as to be beyond rational aesthetic criteria. They are at one with nature, or at least at one with television, with American experience.

Staging the show, as anyone can see from surviving films and kinescopes, was always a spontaneous, audience-responsive occasion. Gleason thought rehearsals were dulling. He can be seen in shot after shot literally pushing the other actors out of his way as he struts and frets his half hour upon the stage; even the rudimentary blocking was done impromptu. Watching *The Honeymooners* now, one sees not a canned, sweetened, homogenized sitcom, but a raw, authentic, preserved performance—an opening night. It still seems oddly live, certainly more so than many a modern-day sitcom taped mere weeks ago in Hollywood.

While *The Honeymooners* got, and continues to get, the most attention, Gleason's gallery was full of invention and inspiration, from the indigent Poor Soul to the profligate Reginald Van Gleason III; from the meek Fenwick Babbitt to the oafish Charlie Bratton. They all fought the establishment, to some extent; they were all Gleason, ritually battling his way out of poverty all over again.

Even Reggie, the dippy dipso millionaire, was a rebel—a traitor to his class who toppled dowagers and insulted his snobbish, wealthy parents. His interests were confined mainly to chorines, booze, and avoiding work. He was the consummate playboy. Reggie's entrances were always the same and always grand: He would burst into a room in flowing opera cape, thirty-gallon stovepipe hat, and shocked anchovie mustache, while Ray Bloch and the house band blasted out a bombastic chorus of "Shangri-la."

It *was* Shangri-la.

Gleason thought Reggie would be the character that would last the longest. He was obviously wrong about that. Ralph and Alice will apparently be squabbling and shouting and kissing and making up ("Baby, you're the greatest") unto infinity. However determinedly Ralph inflated himself into pomposity, Alice was always there with the remedial needle: "Now that you've got your gasbag filled, why don't you blow away?"

Most of Alice's withering put-downs had to do with Ralph's weight. When he said of his latest scheme that it was the biggest thing he ever got into, she said, "The biggest thing you ever got into was your pants." Gleason, though he was known to weigh as much as 280 pounds, said he never thought of himself as a "fat guy," and so was never bothered by the leveling insults with which the writers armed Alice. Gleason may have been fat, but he remained remarkably agile. He ran, careened, tumbled, pratfell, and cartwheeled. After proclaiming, "And away we go!," he would do a mad dance across the stage to "That's A-Plenty." As

Reggie, Gleason would launch into wild, prolonged terpsi-chorean digressions.

In *The Hustler*, Paul Newman as Fast Eddie watches Gleason as pool kingpin Minnesota Fats and says in awe, "Look at the way he moves—like a dancer!"

Over his years on TV, Gleason contributed many a catch-phrase to pop lingo of the time. Ralph's ritual frivolous threat to Alice started out as "One of these days, Alice, one of these days, pow! Right in the kisser," and evolved to a shorthand version about launching her into outer space: "To the moon," and "Bang, zoom!" But most of the catchphrases were positive, elated, celebratory. "Ooo, you're a good group," he would tell the studio audience. "You're a dan-dan-dandy." Reggie followed every eye-popping swig of hootch with an appreciative, "Mmm, that's good booze." Later in his TV years, Gleason could get an approving ovation from the Miami Beach crowd merely by de-claring, "How sweet it is."

How sweet what was? How sweet life was, that's what he meant.

Audrey Meadows looks back on her years with Gleason as frenzied but joyful. She remembers that no crisis fazed him even if it happened one minute before airtime. She remembers being called down to his dressing room before a show to share one of the huge pizzas he'd had trucked in from the Bronx. She remem-bers getting calls from Gleason's valet late at night asking her for a recipe that Gleason had particularly liked.

And she remembers the last time she ever heard his voice.

"I talked to him on the phone, on a Monday. He was gone on Wednesday. He was so sick. Marilyn said, 'I'm going to take the phone in to him. His speech isn't very clear, but I'll put you on.' So I heard her say, as she took the phone to the bed, 'Jackie, it's Audrey. It's your Alice.'

"I said, 'Jackie, I just called to tell you I loved you.' And he said something—I didn't understand a word of it, his speech was slurred so. And I said, 'I never thanked you for giving me the part of Alice.' And suddenly he said, 'I knew what I was doing!' The same voice as ever, clear as a bell."

Meadows balked when producers of the Emmy Awards show entreated her to appear on the telecast in 1987 as Alice and deliver a "eulogy" to Ralph Kramden. "I said, 'I think that is the worst thing I have ever heard in my entire life. I cannot imagine anything worse.' I said, "In the first place, Ralph is not dead.

" 'Ralph will live forever.' "

The biggest thing Jackie Gleason ever got into was television. It became bigger for having him in it; it got smaller when he left. He was big news, a hero, a hee-RO! There were plenty of tributes and retrospectives in the months after he died. The ones that count most are probably the private, personal ones, like when you're sitting in front of the tube late at night and suddenly Gleason is there—as Ralph, as Reggie, as Fenwick or Charlie, or as himself—and you laugh or cry or are caught somewhere in between.

Gleason was asked how he reacted when he saw an old *Honeymooners* after years away from the show. "I never laugh at me," he said. "But I *die* at what Carney does. That man is gorgeous."

One of Gleason's notable dramatic roles was the cynical, worldly Joe in a live *Playhouse 90* version of William Saroyan's *The Time of Your Life.* In the barroom scenes, Gleason's glass was filled, and refilled, with real champagne; he was not a halfway kind of guy. From available evidence, it appears Jackie Gleason had the time of his life, too. But the idea was to give us the time of ours.

A boy wonder to the very end, and of how many boys can that be said?

And then, as it must to all men, death came to George Orson Welles.

Half a century ago, Orson Welles made what is now considered at least the greatest American film, maybe the greatest film, period, of all time, and he made it when he was twenty-five years old. *Citizen Kane* was about a legendary figure in history, and before his life was over, the legend of Welles would eclipse the legend of Kane and a lot of other twentieth-century legends one could think of.

He was, indeed, ecliptic. In more ways than one. His later years saw the man who remade cinema with *Kane* and who panicked the country with his Halloween radio prank *The War of the Worlds*, become best known for talk-show appearances

(David Frost once introduced the three-hundred-pounder as "a giant of a man in every way"), and a series of commercials in which he effortlessly played the bon vivant and connoisseur, saying on behalf of the firm that hired him, "We will sell no wine before its time."

Comparisons between Welles and Kane are inevitable. Kane was a man "who got everything he wanted and then lost it," says a character in the film. An unkind biography of Welles was called *The Rise and Fall of an American Genius.* In his twenties, and America's thirties and forties, Welles buzzed brilliantly through the worlds of theater, radio, and then movies; as actor, director, writer, and producer. But though many of his subsequent films earned high places in cineaste pantheons (especially his Shakespearian pastiche *Chimes at Midnight* and the *film noir* thriller *Touch of Evil*), Welles was haunted by the long shadow of *Kane* for the rest of his career.

His youth pursued him and dogged him, somewhat the way Harry Lime, as Welles played him, was pursued and dogged by his dark deeds through the streets of Vienna in Carol Reed's *The Third Man*.

The real curse of *Kane*, though, was that it was not a commercial success. It lost money for the studio, RKO, that, over great objection from William Randolph Hearst—on whom Charles Foster Kane was loosely based—released it. Welles had played the brilliant brat at the studio when making the film. In the BBC's *Tales of Hollywood*, the story of RKO, it was reported that Welles would meet studio chiefs at the soundstage entrance and stall them with magic tricks to prevent them from going inside.

Kane all but disappeared toward the end of the forties, and when *Sight and Sound* magazine polled world critics for their lists of the all-time best films in 1952, *Kane* didn't make the top ten. But the film returned to circulation when the RKO library was sold to television in the fifties, and by 1962, when the poll was taken again, *Citizen Kane* came in first.

Since then, it has probably become the most written-about and argued-about American film, prompting landmark essays from Andrew Sarris in 1956 and Pauline Kael in 1971. Kael tried to shift the major credit for the screenplay from Welles to his inspired collaborator, Herman Mankiewicz. If Welles didn't write it, he still was probably the film's author. After all, even Welles detractor John Houseman—who never forgave Orson for throwing flaming Sterno cans at him one night at Chasen's in Beverly Hills—had said that the character of Kane was as much Welles as it was Hearst.

Kane was asked in the film by his banker what it was he had wanted to be. He told the banker, "Everything you hate." That, perhaps, was Welles talking to the Hollywood Establishment. The soundstage was never big enough, the money never flowed freely enough, the bosses were never forgiving enough. He made a few masterpieces anyway.

In Hollywood, the town without pity, Welles could be seen often in his last years at Ma Maison, a plain-plush restaurant then on Melrose Avenue, where Orson berthed for lunch. Welles's arrivals down a long, shrub-lined walkway leading to the front door were ceremonial. He moved, it was observed, like an ocean liner going through the St. Lawrence Seaway.

Occasionally, he would suffer the presence of journalists. One later told the story that upon arriving at the restaurant for an appointment with Welles and finding him already moored, he sat down for lunch and an interview. When the check came and was handed to the journalist, there were three lunches billed instead of two. Welles had arrived an hour early, eaten a first lunch, and then stayed for another.

He was a man of enormous appetites as well as multi talents. Sent to Rio by RKO to make a feature after *Kane,* Welles squandered the studio's money and logged a record of sexual adventures still spoken of in wonder.

To behold Welles in the flesh was patently unforgettable. Once, in Hollywood, he agreed to appear at a screening of snippets from one of his innumerable uncompleted films, *The Other Side of the Wind.* Other members of the panel sat in chairs at the front of the Directors Guild of America, where the screening was held. In the middle was one chair twice the size of the others. It was a mammoth, overstuffed, upholstered easy chair. There was no question about who would be sitting there.

I jumped at the chance, when asked, to appear on a late-night news program to discuss a controversial TV movie, *Special Bulletin,* with Orson Welles, who was to be piped in from Los Angeles. The TV show borrowed fake-out techniques from Welles's *War of the Worlds.* The chance to meet Welles even electronically was too good to pass up. I sat in the Washington bureau before the taping, waiting for Welles to arrive in the L.A. studio.

Finally, on a small speaker mounted on the floor, I heard the voice of Orson Welles, that mighty Wurlitzer boom, speaking my name. This was the voice I had heard saying "Rosebud," and warning that the Martians had landed in New Jersey. This was how the voice of God would probably sound if it came over the radio.

Welles hobnobbed with royalty, married goddesses (among them, Rita Hayworth), and could recite from memory all of King Lear's speeches at the age of seven. According to legend, he sat up in his crib when he was eighteen months old and remarked to a doctor visiting the Welles home, "The desire to take medicine is the greatest feature which distinguishes men from animals," either quoting Sir William Osler or coincidentally expressing the very same thought.

He had a glorious youth but a misspent adulthood, or so some may think. But the curse of having made *Citizen Kane* is the kind of affliction to which most of us mortals can only wistfully aspire.

Perhaps someday, a filmmaker of the future will attempt to make *Citizen Welles*. It should be a hoot. Welles almost made his own autobiographical film in his last years: *The Cradle Will Rock,* about Welles's famous Mercury Theater Production of the musical play of the same name. Forbidden by the sponsoring Federal Theater Project from raising the curtain on the left-wing play—authorities actually padlocked the doors to the auditorium where it was to open that night—Welles and his entourage led a crowd that had gathered to another theater, where the actors and composer Mark Blitzstein put on a makeshift performance without benefit of seats or props.

A script for the film was written. Rupert Everett, a brash young British star, was to play Welles. But at the last minute; the backers chickened out. The name of Orson Welles, which had attracted them to the production in the first place, subsequently scared them away.

For all the Shakespeare Welles spoke on stage and screen, the dialogue most associated with him may be Harry Lime's parting speech to his friend Holly, played by Joseph Cotten, in *The Third Man.* They have just stepped off a Ferris wheel.

"Don't be so gloomy," Harry Lime says. "After all, it's not that awful. What the fella said: In Italy for thirty years under the Borgias, they had warfare, terror, murder, bloodshed—but they produced Michelangelo, Leonardo da Vinci, and the Renaissance. In Switzerland, they had brotherly love and five hundred years of democracy and peace, and what did that produce? The cuckoo clock."

"So long, Holly."

And he vanishes into the gloom of day.

From the turbulence of the century he epitomized, Orson Welles fashioned art for the masses, in a style and on a scale no one may ever undertake again. People will search for Orson's "Rosebud," a single image that explains everything. If they ever find it, it will probably be something that was right there under their noses the whole time. A simple thing, like a sled half-buried in snow, or a girl in a white dress glimpsed for a second on the Staten Island Ferry, or a Declaration of Principles, or your first report card at school.

For as long as people watch movies—his, and everybody else's—they'll be telling tall tales of Orson Welles.

COVER GIRL

he was the Mona Lisa of pinups—not just a seductive image, but the very image of seduction. Bright, lithe, willowy, radiant, Rita Hayworth floated through the movies as if suspended by wires. In the days when movies were larger than life, she was inestimably more beautiful.

Rita Hayworth vanished from the public eye, at least officially, long before her death at the age of sixty-eight. Alzheimer's disease had made her a recluse; sponsors of a charity gala, held in her honor, couldn't have imagined she would actually appear, and she didn't. But the Rita Hayworth created by the play of light upon a silvery screen still existed, and still exists now—still teases, still charms, still knows how to peel off a long black glove.

She is just out of reach. But she was always just out of reach.

She is illusory and unreal. But she was always illusory and unreal.

Rita Hayworth was a creation, an invention, an idealization produced in the dream factories of the studio system. But this takes nothing away from her. If you're born beautiful, it's an accident, something beyond your control. But for Marguerita Cansino to become Rita Hayworth was a creative—and col-laborative—act, a lofty accomplishment. Not that she started from scratch, of course.

Of all the stars referred to as goddesses, she was the most goddessy. It really wasn't an overstatement when, during his crooning of the title tune from *You Were Never Lovelier,* Fred Astaire looked into her eyes and sang, "Down the sky, the moonbeams fly to light your face. I can only say they chose the proper place."

Hell, *no one* was ever lovelier.

No one believed that offscreen she lived a life as dreamily glamorous as the one she lived onscreen. But clearly it was a colorful existence. Her five husbands included the brat genius Orson Welles, who starred with her in *The Lady from Shanghai,* and, once Welles was orbited, Aly Khan, whom she married in 1949.

American boys carried her intoxicating glossy into combat during World War II, and the story goes that her photo was affixed to the first atomic bomb dropped on Japan.

How great an actress she was is probably, and was probably, irrelevant, although she certainly did scorch up the screen in *Gilda,* particularly during the famous "Put the Blame on Mame" number. She removed only a long black glove, but her then-daring cleavage and the power of suggestion established the routine as a new audacious high in screen sexiness. It was a cheerful, playful sexiness that glistened and shimmered. There was no point in putting up any resistance.

Her dancing with Astaire in their two movies together (the

other was *You'll Never Get Rich*) wasn't just passable; it was damn good. In the "Shorty George" number from *You Were Never Lovelier*, with Hayworth wearing a brief tennis outfit, she was ecstatically watchable. Hayworth was the only one of all Fred Astaire's dancing partners who outclassed him on the screen—not outdanced him, but outclassed him.

During her years at Columbia, when Hayworth was considered one of the few forces on earth that could tame notorious studio boss Harry Cohn, she starred with Gene Kelly in the very Technicolored *Cover Girl*, and she was a knockout in shot after fussed-over shot. "We're a wonderful pair," says Kelly in one scene. "Aren't we though?" she says back to him.

Though her singing voice was dubbed by someone else, it was such a gossamer, crystalline sound that it might as well have been coming from her. We could accept that. In *Cover Girl*, she cooed nostalgically into Kelly's ear and ours, "Long ago, and far away, I dreamed a dream one day," and he refrained, "Chills run up and down my spine, Aladdin's lamp is mine."

She appeared in biblical kitsch and action-adventure and *films noirs* and, before Cohn told her to dye her hair red, a John Wayne B-western or two. Though her real name was indeed exotic, she was born in Brooklyn—almost, but not quite, a Latin from Manhattan.

After *Gilda* she tended to play mostly women wronged or gone wrong, or both, among them the eponymous heroine of *Miss Sadie Thompson* and a stripper-turned-socialite in *Pal Joey*, which included another burlesque number—called "Zip"—that wasn't quite the torrid showstopper that "Mame" had been. But if a show needed stopping, Hayworth could do it. On her first appearance in a film, you needed a few seconds just to stare at her and take her in. You wished you could have sung to her the way Astaire did.

In *Cover Girl,* the young actress she plays is invited at one point (by Lee Bowman) to try out a vast empty stage for size. She twirls around under a spotlight, her dress billowing out, her fabulous bare shoulders spinning, a joyously unattainable vision. One could attain it for only two hours at a time.

During the big production number, she descends a huge streamlined ramp in a gold dress and into the arms of waiting chorus boys who toss her about, chase her about, and fling her to and fro. Ever elusive, ever evanescent, she escapes them all and dances back up the ramp into a studio-made heaven of hovering clouds. What an exit. If only she'd been able to leave real life in such appropriately celestial style.

At the end of the film, she and Kelly and Phil Silvers, three pals, charge out of a friendly oyster bar and into the night air of a fabricated New York, joining in a chorus that goes, "Let's keep on singing make way for tomorrow; the sun is bringing a new day tomorrow." A wind machine ruffles her long, lustrous hair. She laughs, she dances, and the music swells.

Another couple of seconds and the lights have come up; the dream is over. Rita Hayworth is just a memory. Oh, but what a memory.

Oh, but what a dream.

INCURABLE YOUTH

hen a movie star dies, all kinds of memories swirl—not only of screen roles and whatever part of the star's private life went public, but also of ways these distant visions and separate lives interacted with our own. In the fifties, Natalie Wood was an ultimate idealized teenager to girls who wanted to be like her and to boys who may have found in her one of their first raging erotic fixations.

She stayed beautiful, she stayed gorgeous; she was never merely a sex kitten, and yet it would be hard to sustain the contention that she was a great actress. Like others who make mysteriously indelible impressions on the mind and dream-life of the mass audience, she was a great movie star—on occasion, a scintillating presence, and Hollywood royalty for the first rock 'n' roll generation.

And even though millions grew up with her, and watched her grow up on the screen, she seemed incurably youthful and, at heart, incorrigibly naughty—the good girl with the bad girl inside. Her death at the age of forty-three, apparently by drowning, seemed all the sadder and more of a cheat because of that youthfulness, and yet it ensured that there would never be a photographic image of her, anywhere, in which she looked old or spent or without that ingenuous insouciance.

Movies can bestow not only immortality of a sort, but eternal youth of a sort.

Although not a particularly potent box-office force in the seventies and eighties, Wood remained within the peripheral vision of the public eye, and repeatedly would snap back into focus. In a 1979 remake of *From Here to Eternity,* she was the principal and perhaps sole source of electricity as she played the sex-starved wife of an army officer at Pearl Harbor in 1941. Her dark Russian eyes were beckoningly provocative, and the film's first scene was one in which she sauntered teasingly across the army base, followed religiously by men's admiring eyes.

She could still be the best of the bad girls.

Natalie Wood made the transition not only from child star to national teenager, but from ingenue to leading lady. In the forties, she appeared to be 20th Century–Fox's answer to MGM's enormously popular Margaret O'Brien when she played the trusting little girl who melts a cynical mother's heart in *Miracle on 34th Street,* the Santa Claus movie now making annual holiday appearances on local television.

Then, in the mid-fifties, she played the teenager fascinated by the enigmatic broodings of James Dean—she was a surrogate for all the girls in the audience—in *Rebel Without a Cause,* which helped galvanize a generation and give it an identity. She looked up at Dean with the same worshipful eyes with which she'd looked up at Santa, but now there was something new in them.

By the time of her best film, *Splendor in the Grass* (1961), she was ready to leave the ranks of adolescence with one last histrionic display—a sensational bathtub scene in which, as a lovestruck high school student, she responds to her mother's obsessive anxiety over her virginity with shrieks and splashes and shouts. It was a shocker, especially after a series of innocuous roles. The film was set in the past, but it and the performances confirmed to every kid who saw it the great truth of youth: that adults know nothing about love.

In 1976, Wood and her movie-magazine husband, Robert Wagner, visited Washington to promote an upcoming TV production of *Cat on a Hot Tin Roof* in which they appeared with Laurence Olivier. It was a poor show, but Wood looked magnificent in a silk slip as Maggie the Cat.

In their hotel room, the couple, who had once divorced and later—as if to obey a plebiscite of movie fans—remarried, ate gooey Reuben sandwiches and talked in pleasingly superficial terms about their lives and careers. They radiated well-being and the Hollywood version of style; they still seemed entranced by how well they looked together and how their romance had assumed the storybook qualities of a mushy movie.

Wood wore a white suit that day, and gold chains around her neck—from one of which dangled a plump red heart—and her deep brown eyes were completely outlined in black, so that they were the first things you saw when you walked into the room, and would have been even if a brass band had been playing in one corner. There was chitchat about family life in Beverly Hills and about show business. She was saucy, and shiny, and down to earth.

She said she couldn't remember all the films she had made, especially those of her childhood. "Even though I don't really remember *Tomorrow Is Forever* in 1946, I remember Orson Welles and Claudette Colbert very vividly," she said, smiling. "Tab Hunter and I did one called *The Burning Hills,* and I had to do this hilarious line [lapsing into a mock-Spanish accent], 'You doity gringos! You turn dees town into a scorpions' nest.' " She laughed. "That makes us break up so much, we'd hate to see the movie disappear."

And she recalled having just shown *Miracle on 34th Street* to her own children, denying a published report that they'd hated the film. "No, they just got a little bored. The only people terribly moved by it were our parents. When the lights came up, there were tears streaming down their cheeks." Wagner was asked then if there was anything about his life with Natalie Wood that he would like to change. He said, "Not a thing that I can think of."

It's hard to watch reruns of *Splendor in the Grass* now and not become even more depressed than the movie is supposed to make you anyway, especially in the last scene, when Wood's voice is heard on the soundtrack—over a shot of her leaving behind the one great love of her life—reciting lines from Wordsworth:

"Though nothing can bring back the hour, of splendor in the grass, of glory in the flower;/We will grieve not, rather find strength in what remains behind."

When she was thirty-eight, Natalie Wood was asked what she thought she would be like when she grew old. "I don't really think that far ahead," she said.

o problem finding Rosalind Russell at the airport that night. She was standing out in the street with her luggage at her side, assertive as a Paris traffic cop. Talk about being true to one's image. Cabs and buses could just go around her. And did.

The plan was to pick her up and take her into town, and her hotel, using the longest route possible, so as to prolong the time for an interview in the backseat. Eventually, though, as the car crawled around Washington, occasionally retracing its tracks, she got wise to the ploy. She interrupted herself mid-reminiscence to bark at the driver, "Say, how're we going—by way of Albany?"

Albany! That was her destination, never achieved, in the classic movie comedy *His Girl Friday*, with Russell as reporter Hildy Johnson and Cary Grant as editor Walter Burns. It was a reworking of a Hecht–MacArthur play in which Hildy had been a man. Many of the women Rosalind Russell played on the screen wore tailored suits; they were tough, bossy, ferociously independent. But they weren't mannish. They were womannish. They were humannish.

Her forty-year screen career included prize parts like the title character of *Craig's Wife*, a manipulative snob; and the very unmarried Rosemary, spinster schoolteacher, in William Inge's *Picnic*. But the roles that fit her best had padded shoulders; they were blunt and breezy dames who could set men straight, or at least bring them up short, with a smart, tart crack or a withering gaze.

That's who Rosalind Russell was: a puncher, a jabber, a scrapper. The Great American Gal, winner and still champion.

"Sad to say, I was never a sex symbol in films, which always irritated me," she said. And she tended to dodge the badge of feminist heroine that some tried to pin on her for parts that seem trailblazing in retrospect. Those roles were all stamped, she said, out of the same "Alice in Careerland" mold.

"My wardrobe had a set pattern. A tan suit, a gray suit, a beige suit, and then a negligee for the seventh reel, near the end, when I would admit to my best friend on the telephone that what I really wanted was to become a dear little housewife."

A pivotal part for her, Russell said, was that of a duplicitous gossip in the movie version of Clare Booth Luce's play *The Women*. Appropriately enough, she had to fight to get it. "The producers told me I was too beautiful for the part. I said, 'Attractive, yes, but beautiful? Never!' I told them I would go down to makeup and have them put six warts on my face if they wanted me to."

The fighting didn't end when she got the part. The film's most famous scene called for a frenzied wrestling match between

Russell and Paulette Goddard, another *femme formidable*. Russell said the scene was filmed in one take and that she was shocked when the camera stopped rolling to look down and see blood on Goddard's leg—at the spot where Russell had bitten it. "I could still see my teeth marks," she recalled. "I guess we got carried away."

In *His Girl Friday*, the brawling was mostly verbal. The scene in which Hildy tackled a cop to the ground was handled by a stunt double. But some of the insults and quips Russell traded with Cary Grant were ad-libbed on the set, Russell said. These protracted spats opened up a witty new front in the battle of the sexes. In this matchup, both sides were equally armed. He may have been prettier than she was; she had the spine and the moxie.

In the later stages of Russell's career, another plum part came her way, the campy Auntie Mame, figment of the imagination of author Patrick Dennis. The film version seems long and cumbersome now, but Russell still sparkles as the rebellious bohemian whose credo was "Live, live, live" and who stopped mid-climb of a grand curving staircase to tell her little nephew, "Oh, what times we're going to have!" Others succeeded Russell as Mame when the film became a stage musical and then a screen musical, but no one approached Russell's performance.

She owned the role and it, in a way, owned her, since most of the other women she played subsequently seemed variations on it. She was asked to carry more than her share in a number of weak vehicles, but then she extended her career again by going onstage and talking about it in a series of personal appearances punctuated with film clips. She had legs, and knew how to use them; the clips included the raucous "Conga" number from the TV version of her Broadway smash *Wonderful Town*, with Russell being tossed around by visiting Greek sailors.

In 1972, she was named by Richard Nixon to the National Council for the Arts, and was seated at a luncheon table near Clint Eastwood, then just becoming a movie star. To Russell, he was a nice young man with whom she flirted shamelessly. He blushed. She teased. There was no doubt who had the upper hand here.

She appeared genuinely to enjoy playing Great Lady of the Screen and spinning her tales of Hollywood, in appearances at Town Hall in New York, the Kennedy Center in Washington, and other venues. Drugs taken for chronic rheumatism made her face look puffy, and she may have had only a passing resemblance to the tall and slender woman on the screen, but the feistiness in the eyes was still there, and it traveled easily past the footlights.

One still had the feeling she could lick any man in the house, and that she wouldn't have to turn submissive in the seventh reel, either. Rosalind Russell had a few bows to take before she went, and she took them with gusto—not so much to settle old scores as to revisit past triumphs. What times she had.

SONG OF THE THIN MAN

f you can keep your dignity in Hollywood, you've really accomplished something. William Powell managed that, and went on from there. He kept his dignity on the screen and, from available reports, in real life as well. Upon his death at the age of ninety-one, the presiding physician said, "The old gentleman went very nicely."

He never seemed a particularly young gentleman on the screen; he didn't play waifs or sprites even when starting out. He always conveyed a maturity, a worldliness, and he was incontestably dapper. William Powell could stride through a whole movie and never unbutton his coat. And that seemed perfectly normal.

His best-remembered films are the *Thin Man* series for MGM—in which he was partnered with an acerbic, jaundiced-eyed Myrna Loy—and pictures like *My Man Godfrey, The Great Ziegfeld, Life with Father,* and his last, *Mister Roberts,* released in 1955. In that one, he shared CinemaScopic quarters with scene-stealers James Cagney, Jack Lemmon, and Henry Fonda, but Powell's performance as the heavily imbibing ship's doctor holds up at least as well as any of them.

That's because in that role he left the screen as he had so often held it, with fabulous understatement.

In many of his films, he was a rogue in a dinner jacket. He was a pipe and slippers, a cigarette holder, blue glass and liquor from decanters. The *Ile de France* with all the gulls around it.

Powell's pseudo-aristocratic bearing and the brittle, teeth-clenched way in which he spoke made him the perfect drawing-room detective. This or that mystery was wrapped up with crisp efficiency and dispatched forthwith. Nick Charles, the nominally retired detective Powell played in the six *Thin Man* movies, was no rumpled gumshoe. He detected as a hobby, the way some men invent cocktails or wade into swamps in hopes of bagging ducks.

Murders in movies were civilized affairs in those days, practically catered ones. A knife in the back, and not a drop of blood. Nick and Nora Charles dealt with these immaculate crimes in an immaculate way. But what the *Thin Man* films also had was a cheeky, ingratiating impudence; the Charles marriage was a battle of wits. Few images so succinctly convey the essence of thirties comedy as a scene from the first *Thin Man* in which Powell's Nick Charles, reclining on the couch, shoots the ornaments off a Christmas tree with the new gun his wife has given him.

Powell actually played several detecting gents, among them Philo Vance, even before MGM teamed him with Loy for *The Thin Man*. A list of his early talkies is also a list of murder cases: *The Canary Murder Case*, *The Greene Murder Case*, *The Benson Murder Case*, *The Kennel Murder Case*. You had a murder case, you called William Powell.

Powell's thirties films bring the era back now in sardonic relief for modern-day movie audiences. Films starring Powell are among the most-requested titles at the American Film Institute Theater in Washington's Kennedy Center for the Performing Arts. "Our audience loves him," says Ray Barry, director of theater operations. When the AFI Theater booked all six *Thin Man* films during the summer of 1982, it registered the largest attendance of any series in the theater's history up to that time.

People may gravitate to William Powell in these films because the sight of him is nostalgic without being at all sappy. He had no cheap tricks to win an audience's empathy; the characters he played were often aloof and even imperious, yet he somehow made them accessible, as if he were the millionaire playboy next door. In *My Man Godfrey*, a seminal Depression-era comedy, Powell was himself the perfect lampooner of snooty airs and rich fops.

Through these films and others—the lesser forties farces *Mr. Peabody and the Mermaid* and *The Senator Was Indiscreet*— Powell epitomized sophistication and chic irreverence. In *Song of the Thin Man,* the last of the series, Nora tells a natty Nick, "You look like a page out of *Esquire,*" and so he does. Asked where he'd left his bottle of scotch, he replies, "In my red pajamas." But of course.

Like Cary Grant, Powell was able to wax suave on the screen without losing status as hero, even folk hero, to the audience. He was dashing, that's what he was. Men could be dashing then. Pianos weren't the only things that were grand.

Critics generally hoot at *The Great Ziegfeld*, an overstuffed musical biography of the famous theatrical producer and show-girl glorifier, but the movie has a friendly hugeness to it now, and it was so enormously popular in its day that Powell was entreated to return to the role of Florenz Ziegfeld, in 1945, to introduce a sequel of sorts, *Ziegfeld Follies,* essentially a revue of musical and comedy acts.

As that picture opens, Powell as Ziegfeld is in heaven, reminiscing about his lavish stage productions. Heaven, in this case, and this being MGM, was a penthouse suite in the stratosphere surrounded by fluffy white billows. Proper attire was a silk smoking jacket. Powell may have behaved nothing at all like Ziegfeld, but he made the character another of his elegant studies in style.

The only way to bring the Ziegfeld character back for *Follies* was to show him in heaven, because he had died at the conclusion of *The Great Ziegfeld,* breathing his last as he slumped in a chair near a window, conjuring up one more Broadway spectacular and murmuring instructions to an imaginary set designer: "I need more steps. I've got to get higher, higher!"

Then his hand fell to his side and he dropped a flower, which in the movie vocabulary of the time meant life had left his body. He had died, but not without panache. A penthouse and silk smoking jacket awaited him. But of course.

He walked so close to the wall as he came down the hotel hallway that he was almost gliding along it. In one hand was his violin case; the other arm swung at his side. Jack Benny looked like a little kid on his way to a junior high school orchestra rehearsal.

Inside the suite, he presided over a press lunch, comporting himself less like a comedian than like an audience. He didn't tell jokes, that's for sure. He could have been somebody's nice uncle, in from out-of-town. Tom Donnelly, a local wit, brought up the subject of overstated rave reviews, the kind where critics claim an audience was so beside itself with delight that "people were throwing babies out of the balcony."

Something about that phrase set Benny off. He completely surrendered to laughter. He slapped the table, hard, three times with his right hand and exploded in big, uninhibited haw-haws.

Then he repeated the line and hawed some more. His reaction became much funnier than the object of it, and soon everybody had joined in. Jack Benny had reverted to childhood; he had the raw enthusiasms of a six-year-old. You got the feeling this mad transformation could overcome him at any moment.

Obviously Jack Benny loved laughter whichever side of it he was on. The music of that laughter carried him through five decades of reliable service to the American people. All those years were funnier because Jack Benny was rooting around in them.

The courageous brunt of almost all his own jokes, Jack Benny portrayed a meticulously detailed character called "Jack Benny"—a vain, petty, conceited, parsimonious despot. He lied about his age, threw temper tantrums at underlings, and pinched pennies until they bled. This was a work in progress, one always being supplemented and refined, and the audience was called upon regularly to render verdicts on new embellishments, the way a patron of the arts might study the progress of a mural, or a chapel ceiling. It was a hilarious and merciless parody of human behavior, one that wore well through decades of radio and television.

Jack Benny was able to make a joke of wearing a toupee long before he really wore one, and on the radio, where it couldn't be seen anyway. He made a joke of his baby-blue eyes on black-and-white TV, proving that television required some imagination on the part of the audience after all. True, people now got to see, as well as hear, those by-then cherished characters from radio: Mary Livingstone, Jack's real wife, as his wife; Don Wilson, his announcer, as his announcer; Dennis Day as that "crazy kid," his singer; and the great Eddie "Rochester" Anderson, valet and loyal companion. But just seeing them didn't complete the picture. You had to bring all your years of enjoying Jack

Benny to the experience—the whole rich lode of lore from which Benny's writers fashioned the weekly, ritual whimsy.

These jokes got better as they got older, as few jokes do. No one else could have made the scripts funny the way Jack Benny and his cohorts did. No one could have gotten such big laughs just saying "Gee" and "Well!" and "Now cut that out!" The whole routine became as cheeringly familiar as a pet dog's bark.

A few years after the press lunch and the ceremonial slapping of the table, Benny was back in Washington to give a press conference before a concert. He said, as he had said before, that he thought Jack Benny, Benny Kubelski's stage name, was "the worst name I ever heard," because it was two first names slapped together. And he said his theme song, "Love in Bloom," was "the worst theme song anybody ever had," because it had nothing to do with him. Oh didn't it?

Benny strode onstage to that music about a million times, both arms swinging, walking with swish overconfidence, making himself at home. He could play the silly cad because everybody saw through it and got the joke. Jack Benny was a man who kept his fortune in an underground vault guarded by alligators, paid his staff pittances and would give his faultlessly loyal Rochester one dollar for Christmas, and stood in helpless indecision when a robber posed the immortal demand: "Your money or your life."

He was thinking it over.

It was a living caricature of preening ego—the self-obsessed tot demanding pampering and humoring, and getting it. As punishment, he was beseeched and entreated by nemeses everywhere he went. They brought out the childish temper beneath the childish vanity. Jack Benny satirized impulses all of us knew we had within ourselves. He was the joke and we were the joke. It was shared, special, communal. It was *entre nous*.

On television, Benny could extend the laughs just by turning his head and staring, the visual equivalent of his radio pause. In latter-day comedy specials, he would turn and stare when a monkey made a Bronx cheer, he would turn and stare when a regiment of penguins marched across the stage, he would turn and stare when Mel Blanc, as a monosyllabic Hispanic, answered all questions with "*Sí,*" "Sy," or "Sue." This was pop surrealism at its friendliest.

The Benny stare was worthy of Hamlet, and so there was justice in the fact that Benny played a cheese Hamlet in the classic Ernst Lubitsch comedy *To Be or Not to Be* during the war. It was one of Benny's few respectable films. Out of his biggest flop, *The Horn Blows at Midnight,* a desperate farce, was fashioned another recurring Benny joke. He would be driving into the studio to do his show and discover that the guard at the gate had been the director of *The Horn Blows at Midnight* and was now a broken man (when, in actuality, the director was the celebrated Raoul Walsh).

In mid-1974, the year in which he died, Jack Benny came to Washington again to play another of his benefit concerts. He raised millions for symphony orchestras by slicing away at his helpless fiddle. Yes, it was lousy violin playing. It was the finest lousy violin playing in the world.

Backstage before the show, Benny paced around as though this were opening night—a kid again, facing his first recital. "Now where's my mute?" he'd exclaim suddenly, then jump up to look for it, carrying the violin and bow around the room with him. He wore thick glasses with heavy frames; his liquid eyes swam behind them. "Now where are my notes?" he demanded. "Now I'd better put on my violin glasses right now, so I don't forget it." He took a capsule from a small, round pillbox; a few months later, it was revealed he suffered from inoperable stomach cancer.

Should he wear his black tuxedo coat or his white dinner jacket? Well, which? Everybody had to give an opinion. He opted for black. Once he'd put it on, he plucked at the silk handkerchief that peeked limply out of the pocket. And he asked the rhetorical question, "Now what kind of a lousy handkerchief is this?" Then he broke out laughing at his own neurotic display. He said, "We're a crazy gang, you know that?"

Between practice exercises on the violin and much agitated pacing back and forth, he fielded questions. Did he really think *The Horn Blows at Midnight* was that terrible a movie?

"Yes. Now ask me if I think *To Be or Not to Be* was one of the greatest comedies ever made." Did he? "Yes, and the difference was Lubitsch."

How good a violinist would Jack Benny have been if he had devoted his life to that, instead of to comedy? "I would have been a great one. But the trouble was, I didn't start practicing again until I was sixty-two years old. Now let's say there was such a thing as a miracle, and that I could stop being a comedian and be a great violinist. Five years ago, I wouldn't have done it, but I would now." He was eighty.

Just after Christmas that year, he died. George Burns, his friend for half a century—the guy who could make Benny collapse in laughter with just the flick of a cigar ash—spoke a brief eulogy at the services: "What can I tell you about Jack that you don't know? I can't imagine life without him. I'll miss him very much."

Mary Livingstone was there, and Rochester, and Dennis Day, and Don Wilson. And Milton Berle, George Jessel, Groucho Marx—fellow members of Jewish show-biz royalty. Benny was buried not far from Al Jolson and Eddie Cantor. And Frank Sinatra was there, and James Stewart, and Gregory Peck, and Ronald Reagan. Johnny Carson, who idolized Benny, said later that when he learned of Benny's death, it was one of the few times in his life that he wept.

Benny's cancer was diagnosed only days before his death. Earlier in the year, he'd spent a week at Cedars of Lebanon Hospital, having suffered a dizzy spell just before another of his innumerable charity appearances. As he was being wheeled out of the hospital, reporters rushed forward, and one asked him if he was experiencing any pain. And he replied, "No. I won't have a stomach ache until I get the bill." Pause. Stare. Jack Benny was still in character, and still leading the chorus of laughter directed at himself.

think I'll miss you most of all," Dorothy whispered in the Scarecrow's ear. The Cowardly Lion was funny, the Tin Woodman was dear, but the Scarecrow had soul. Oz wouldn't have been the same without him. The rest of the world won't be the same without Ray Bolger, the lanky and vivacious vaudevillian who played the Scarecrow, his role of roles, in *The Wizard of Oz.*

Bolger was the last surviving star of *The Wizard of Oz*—made in 1939 but never far from the public eye—and even if his appearances grew rare in modern times, you knew he was around, and you felt that, just like you and the kids, he might have been watching the movie during its annual telecasts.

He never expressed anything but gratitude about being known best for this one part, despite the many others he played on stage and screen in his long and rambunctious career. In 1976, he looked back on the film and said, "It's a great American classic, and after I'm gone, it will be—and I will be—remembered. And very few people can say they were remembered for anything in life."

Ray Bolger can be remembered for even more than this well-loved triumph. He electrified Broadway, dancing George Balanchine's *Slaughter on Tenth Avenue* in the finale of Rodgers and Hart's *On Your Toes* in 1936. The dance was constructed to become more and more frenetic, and Bolger said later that he fainted "many times" after his nightly performances.

When he appeared in Frank Loesser's *Where's Charley?*, a Broadway musicalization of *Charley's Aunt*, Bolger had, and made the most of, another fabled showstopper, "Once in Love With Amy," a song so infectious and lilting that audiences began singing along with him. Sometimes, he later recalled, they demanded so many encores that he would finally bring the singing to a halt and announce, "This is a play. We have to finish it!"

"Amy" is a moonstruck anthem to first love. "Once you're kissed by Amy, tear up your list; it's Amy," Bolger sang. In real life, he was once in love with Gwendolyn, always in love with Gwendolyn—Gwendolyn Rickard. They were wed in 1929, and the marriage lasted until Bolger's death.

In person as onstage, Bolger was the picture of ebullience. Even in his seventies, his eyes shined a buoyant, youthful crystalline blue. He was not easily lured into racy gossip about the early days of Hollywood, and he denied stories that the older stars on the set of *Wizard* became irritated when they thought that young Judy Garland was upstaging them.

He started dancing at the age of sixteen, saved from a life in the insurance business by the urge to perform. He learned some of his first steps, he said, from a night watchman who had once been a hoofer. For a time, he toured the vaudeville circuits as half of an act called "Sanford & Bolger, a Pair of Nifties." Roaming New England as a vaudeville performer was, he said later, "my education."

His comic dancing style was his alone, facilitated by a pair of legs that, he was once told, seemed to start under his arms. In films like *The Harvey Girls*, in which he starred with Garland again, he performed singular specialty numbers full of impish, gravity-defying displays worthy of the great silent-movie comics. He knew how to make people smile and how to leave them happy.

His efforts in television, in addition to thirty years of annual telecasts of *The Wizard of Oz*, included an early ABC sitcom called *Where's Raymond?*, in which he played a Broadway hoofer much like himself. More recently, he popped up on the occasional *Love Boat*, or even on sitcoms like *The Partridge Family*. He had tremendous energy, loved to work, and once wrote, "You can never stop learning in television; the medium is limitless."

One Bolger television show was short-lived but memorable, a Sunday afternoon variety hour in the fifties called *Washington Square*. Bolger danced on a studio set made to resemble a Greenwich Village neighborhood. An Italian woman would sing operatic arias from her tenement window. And Bolger introduced a novelty tune, "The Song of the Cricket," that became a national hit.

In 1976, he returned to TV for a straight dramatic role in a remake of John Osborne's bitter play *The Entertainer*, cast as aged ex-vaudevillian Billy Rice. The production was lame, but Bolger was golden. He had a climactic dramatic dance routine that made it all worthwhile.

"People just don't know what entertainment is anymore,"

Billy Rice grumbled. Bolger said he didn't agree with that remark, but with his death, the era of vaudeville and all its dauntless, resourceful troupers fades still further into history. When *The Wizard of Oz* is shown each year, it really is a one-night stand of old pros, a two-hour vaudeville revival, a chance to see and share a form of magic rarely practiced today.

Every child knows that the Scarecrow played by Bolger asks the Wizard of Oz for a brain, not knowing he has had one all along, and is given an honorary degree at the end of his journey: "Th.D., Doctor of Thinkology." Delighted almost beyond words, the Scarecrow puts his finger to his head and declares, "The sum of the square roots of any two sides of an isosceles triangle is equal to the square root of the remaining side."

Then he exclaims, "Oh joy, oh rapture! I've got a brain!" He asks the Wizard, "How can I ever thank you?" and the Wizard replies hurriedly, "Well, you can't." How can we ever thank Ray Bolger? Well, we can't.

To Oz? To Oz!

COURT JESTER

o children of several generations, there was no easy way to say the name "Danny Kaye" without smiling. It became a phrase of magical, liberating associations, like "ice cream." To see him in a performance was to ride a carousel, or sneak into the circus, or spend a Sunday afternoon at the ballpark with Dad. You could have all the hot dogs you wanted.

Danny Kaye didn't start out as primarily a children's entertainer. In the forties, he was considered quite the sophisticated wit with his tongue-twisting patter songs—like "Tchaikovsky," which he sang in *Lady in the Dark.* But then in 1952, he made *Hans Christian Andersen* for Samuel Goldwyn, and he became, as the queen of Denmark said when she knighted him in 1983, "Pied Piper to the children of the world."

On stage or screen, Danny Kaye tried to find the child in you.

He was determined to seek it out and set it free. If you were lucky, he did. The kid got out and ran around and acted silly and nobody told him to behave. Danny Kaye, one may have felt, went over the heads of adults to a higher level of understanding: an innocent's.

It was Kaye's work with the United Nations Children's Fund that earned him the Pied Piper status. CBS News celebrated it in a memorable 1957 edition of *See It Now* called "The Secret World of Danny Kaye." His gratis volunteerism for UNICEF wasn't a secret anymore after that, yet Kaye never seemed to be exploiting that special relationship he had with the young.

In one of his last television appearances, on *The Cosby Show* in late 1985, Kaye worked winningly with the Cosby kids. He was particularly smitten with the youngest, Keshia Knight-Pulliam, who plays Rudy. "He was just overwhelmed by Keshia," director Jay Sandrich said later. "He kept saying, 'I can't believe how good she is.'"

Cosby kept a low profile on this installment of TV's top-rated show and let Kaye work his old spell in the role of a dentist who cheers children out of their fear in the dentist's chair. Kaye was nominated for an Emmy for the role.

"Bill in his own way paid him a lot of homage," Sandrich said. "Danny had his own way of working, but he said, 'I don't want to look different than anybody else.' He wanted to fit into the show. He spent a lot of time with the writers talking about his past experiences.

"I'd grown up as a child with him being my favorite entertainer. We realized how honored we all felt that he was on this show."

"Entertainer" is precisely the word for what Kaye was; headlines referred to him as "Entertainer Danny Kaye." He sang, he danced, he was funny, he was dramatic. You couldn't put him in a category. His talents were many; his mission was to please and amuse and move.

He learned his trade by doing just about everything that could be done in show business of his day. He held fans for fan dancer Sally Rand, and he plunged fully clothed into swimming pools for patrons of Catskill hotels during his days as a "tummler," a kind of resident wacky kept on the premises like a pet.

It all paid off when Kaye became a movie and radio star in the forties and fifties, and it reached a high point during the four-year run of *The Danny Kaye Show* on CBS from 1963 to 1967. The only thing wrong with the show was that CBS foolishly scheduled it for 10:00 P.M., too late for many of the children who should have been watching.

But there was a lot of childlike charm to the hour, which included broad comedic spoofs of operas and ballets and other such deft skewerings of pretentiousness, and which exercised Kaye's knack for dialects of every configuration. Harvey Korman, as he would be later for Carol Burnett, was second banana. Kaye opened and closed the show wafting out from the wings across a vast empty stage, his long arms making him just this side of airborne.

On every show, there was a segment of Danny talking to kids, including one particularly luminous tot named Victoria Meyerink, four years old when the show started. Danny Kaye could really light up a child's eyes. It wasn't just a talent, it was a gift, and the performer got great obvious pleasure from spreading it around.

Kaye's best-known movies included *The Secret Life of Walter Mitty* in 1946 and *White Christmas* in 1954. In the latter film, he and costar Bing Crosby had to do a number called "Sisters" dressed as women. As the story goes, Bing was reluctant but Danny loosened him up, and convinced him to let his hair down.

Bing's laughter during the number in the finished film is real, it's said. Danny provoked it. He provoked a lot of laughter in his forty years of entertaining.

Kaye's seventeen films were uneven, occasionally overproduced (some by Samuel Goldwyn, who ordered Kaye's hair dyed blond), but there were moments of manic brilliance. His slapstick acrobatics in *Walter Mitty*, which included being pushed out of a window by Boris Karloff, were expertly done, but verbal pyrotechnics were as much a Kaye trademark as physical gags. In *The Court Jester* (1956), his last first-class movie, Kaye was wildly funny dueling with Basil Rathbone in a climactic rout, and hilarious in a classic elocutionary exercise with Mildred Natwick built around the cautionary couplet, "The pellet with the poison's in the vessel with the pestle; the chalice from the palace has the brew that is true."

The film opened and closed with Kaye singing, "Life Could Not Better Be," and it couldn't.

Known to be short-tempered, even surly, off-camera and off-stage, Kaye was of a performing generation that believed the audience must never be shortchanged, and so he didn't take kindly to any intimations that it had been. When a flattering fan complained to Kaye after one show that he hadn't been onstage long enough, one Hollywood tale goes, Kaye hauled off and decked him.

What was Danny Kaye's specialty? He was a specialty. The broad smile and the mischievous eyes were invitations to escape and play, to goof off and feel better for it. He didn't dance out of view at the end of his TV shows so much as he dematerialized, an emissary from youth who made invigorating but fleeting visitations.

Many of the songs in *Hans Christian Andersen* became popular children's favorites, like "Thumbelina" and "The Ugly Duckling," but my personal favorite was always "Wonderful, Wonderful Copenhagen," sung by Kaye on a prop ship sailing rear-screen seas toward a painted, glistening vista.

We kids wanted to be standing there too, making this marvelous journey off to a mystical place. When we think of Danny Kaye, we don't think of him standing alone in a spotlight or on a screen, apart and distant; we picture ourselves with him, giggling and cheered and young again. School is out for the summer, and the world is ours.

~~~~~~
~~~~~~
~~~~~~

Jimmy Durante was perhaps the greatest song-and-dance man we ever had who couldn't really sing and didn't quite dance.

Essentially his act was to come onstage and be beloved. He did it so well you could never tell he was trying.

How will we tell the children what Jimmy Durante did? Jokes? He had "a million of 'em," but sensational they were not. Songs? "You gotta start off each day" with one, he sang, but his voice was pure Brillo.

"I got that note from Bing Crosby," he'd exclaim after one lopsided-pear-shaped tone, "and boy, was he glad to get rid of it."

And that dancing of his—it was mainly a strut around the stage, with hat held high, mouth wide open, eyes beaming, nose erect and pointing heavenward. Oh yeah, that was one other thing about him: He had a very big, veritably Cyranovian, nose. But he wasn't always butting it into other people's business.

Durante was boffo in vaudeville, having started at Coney Island in 1910, and he stormed through a number of MGM musicals, often tweaking high-hats like Lauritz Melchior. On radio, he was a smash with Garry Moore. But it was television that made him most accessible to the most millions, extending his career as it extended the careers of many other great vaudevillians.

If vaudeville had died, someone said, television was the box it was buried in. But it wasn't dead. Eddie Cantor, Ed Wynn, Durante, and other old-timers brought it back for one more life. Television was the hereafter.

Milton Berle, another incurable ham, had bombed on radio but became Mr. Television; he once said that a career's worth of material could be used up in a few weeks of TV exposure. But these entertainers came out of traditions so hardy and experience so seasoned that they managed to add years to their professional longevities. It didn't matter if Jimmy Durante blew a line during a comedy sketch, because he could make recovering from the fluff so funny.

One knew precisely what to expect of George Burns and Gracie Allen, week after week on CBS, but those expectations were fulfilled with imagination and pizzazz. It was never precisely a shock when Jimmy Durante yelled, "Stop the music!" in mid-song, or began the systematic demolition of a piano, or shouted, "This is a catastra-stroaf!" We knew what he was going to do. We also knew nobody else could do it.

From out of the wings of the studio, of vaudeville, and of memory, he would bring his former partner Eddie Jackson for a two-thirds resurrection of the team of Clayton, Jackson, and Durante. Most of those watching in the television audience had never heard of Clayton, Jackson, and Durante (Lou Clayton died in 1950), yet we all felt as though we had. Or should have. It was part of our tribal memory, back there, somewhere. What was precisely the charm of it? It's hard to say, but it was precisely charming.

There was always a sentimental undercurrent to Durante's performances, and he was persistently endearing for the pose he struck—that of the Brooklyn wiseacre, up from poverty, rubbing elbows with the bigwigs (bringing cultural nabobs like Helen Traubel and Ethel Barrymore down to, or maybe up to, his level), a raucous incorrigible who took arms against a sea of pomposities and, by opposing, sank them.

The big assault on the old heartstrings came at the end of his show, at least the biweekly half hour that alternated with Donald O'Connor's on NBC. Jimmy the Well-Dressed Man, the defiantly homely cuss who never complained about the barbs hurled at his proboscis, bid adieu to the camera, the audience, and a mythical long-lost love and walked off into four pools of light that trailed into darkness. Whence, fortnightly, he would return.

In a trademark battered hat (he had lots of trademarks), Durante sang a good-night song: "We've had a few laughs, now it's time for toodle-oo. Au revoir [pronounced Oh-re-voe], auf wiedersehn and inka-dinka-doo. . . ." Inka-dinka-doo? That was another of his trademarks—a song that went "Ink, a dinka-dink, a dinka-dink . . ." What does it mean? According to the lyrics, it "simply means ink, a-dinka dink, a dinka doo."

So, anyway, the song also observed, with a near-tantric redundancy, "Good night, good night, good night. There's nothing left to say but good night." Then Durante would say, "Good night, folks—and good night, Mrs. Calabash, wherever you are."

It was much ado about adieu, all right. But it worked every week, a sweet, simple benediction with which to conclude thirty minutes of rampage. The anarchic streak in Durante's comedy was always under control; it was a cordial anarchic streak. And a narrow one. He was the rambunctious kid who'd crashed a Park Avenue party and, by the time it was over, had won every heart in the place.

Durante had several careers, most of them dependent on his irreverent and audacious appearance. Suppose he'd been born with a normal-size shnozzola, what then? Everything would have turned out pretty much the same.

In one last career, in the sixties and seventies, Durante played Pagliaccio. He became, for a few years, a best-selling recording artist, and not with comedy albums or gag tunes, either. He recorded collections of rueful ballads about growing old, and looking backward, loving and losing, and *temps perdu.* The raspy voice and fractured phonetics didn't impede the effectiveness of numbers like "September Song"; they enhanced it. A song previously taken for granted might assume a nutty new poignance, as when Durante trilled:

"And here is de best part, you have a head start, if you are amongst de very young at heart."

He was amongst 'em. Always.

Whatever Durante did, it was entertainment for entertainment's sake, not in the interest of producing serious side effects. He was totally apolitical and happily irrelevant, and you could trust him on that. If he'd taken up partisan causes or lent himself to missions, it might have seemed a form of betrayal. About the most political thing he ever uttered on the record was said during the acrimonious turmoil of the sixties. Durante is supposed to have asked the rhetorical question, "Why can't everybody leave everybody else the hell alone?"

There's nothing left to say but "good night."

Good night, good night, good night.

A SOUL OF HIS OWN

~~~~~~
~~~~~~

enry Fonda stood up to bullies. He didn't usually
shoot them, as John Wayne did, but he stood up to
them. He confronted them, he talked them down, he
shamed them into submission. There never has been
a shortage of bullies for the shaming.

And because Henry Fonda did that in some of his
best movies, he came to epitomize the proud, tough, lean, in-
dividualist who sticks to his principles so firmly they become part
of his skin. Henry Fonda symbolized some of the aspects of the
American character that we prize most, and there is reason to
believe he tried to bring those qualities to his personal life as well.
Nobody wanted to see him knuckle under in the movies. And
no one wanted to see him knuckle under to his own mortality,
his own deteriorating health, in real life.

As Tom Joad, the oppressed Everyman of John Steinbeck's

The Grapes of Wrath, Fonda promised he would be around forever, and in roles like that, he will be.

From his sinewy portrayal of *Young Mr. Lincoln* in 1939, to the role of the cantankerous, death-defying Norman Thayer of *On Golden Pond* in 1981, Fonda was the picture of resolve on the screen.

He became emblematic of the frontier traits it has often been said this country was built on: independence, determination, grit, and stubbornness. He was steadfast. As the lone dissenter at a lynching party in *The Ox-Bow Incident*, he spoke out against mob justice. As the lone dissenter on a hanging jury in *Twelve Angry Men* fourteen years later, he spoke out for the rights of a wrongly accused man.

As the president of the United States in *Fail Safe*, in 1964, Henry Fonda somehow made it seem reasonable to sacrifice the city of New York when U.S. missiles accidentally wiped out Moscow in the course of a colossal cold-war snafu.

He made many films that were not successful, and he proved his versatility by playing a wide variety of characters, but he was at his best when, as might have been said of him in a detracting way, "he was always the same." Not just in the sense of his trade-marked, tight-lipped, midwestern-twanged delivery, either. It became with Fonda less a matter of acting than a matter of being what people wanted him to be. The camera smiled on him as it did on a few others of his generation, and turned him into something more, in the mass mind, than an actor, and something more than a movie star. He was lucky enough to become a symbol, one that could survive box-office clinkers or the occasionally embarrassing public utterances of children Peter and Jane.

Fonda and his "image" grew so inseparable that when he finally was given an Oscar for a performance (one year after receiving an "honorary" one), it was generally acknowledged that the trophy was less kudos for *On Golden Pond*, with its slim conceit and banal characters, than an expression of gratitude for a life's work. It was the Henry Fonda Award for being Henry Fonda.

Only Fonda himself could know how much fortitude it took to keep working after repeated hospitalizations, heart surgery, the implanting of a pacemaker, and other infirmities. It must have taken plenty—courage or just ornery defiance, which is what we expected Fonda to stand for on the screen. In one of his last performances, a TV movie called *Gideon's Trumpet*, he played Clarence Earl Gideon, the impoverished Florida man who, when sent to prison, learned enough law there to challenge his conviction and help establish the precedent that every accused person is entitled to legal counsel. Gideon thereby got a new stature, one even history books couldn't bestow, because he was being played by Henry Fonda.

In a way, Gideon was kin to Tom Joad. And to Mr. Roberts, whom Fonda played on the stage and the screen and who made a heroic act of standing up to a tyrannical navy captain obsessed with a palm tree. And to Wyatt Earp, played by Fonda in the classic 1946 John Ford western *My Darling Clementine*, which had Fonda setting a whole town on the straight and narrow.

It was in that film that Fonda made something curiously indelible out of a simple scene in which Earp sat on a front porch, leaned back in his chair, and did a little dance with his feet on the railing. It's one of those tiny moments that, once seen, is not forgotten. The film, meant as a celebration of Americana, is now Americana itself, of another era in filmmaking that celebrated decency and heroism. Fonda had a way of making simple decency look complex. And now he is as much a part of Americana as the characters he played.

Perhaps Tom Joad was right when he said he would always be "there"—at least in the sense that a part of him was usually there in a Fonda performance. In the late sixties, at a dinner honoring

Fonda and recalling *The Grapes of Wrath*, author Steinbeck remembered first seeing Fonda in the role of Joad. "A lean, stringy, dark-faced piece of electricity walked out on the screen, and he *had* me," Steinbeck said. "I believed my own story again. It was fresh and happening and good. Hank can do that."

Steinbeck called Fonda "devoted, hard-working and responsible, with a harsh urge toward perfection" and said he thought of him as "a man reaching but unreachable, gentle but capable of sudden and dangerous violence, sharply critical of others, but equally self-critical, caged, and fighting the bars, but timid of the fight. . . ."

Producer Darryl F. Zanuck was said to have written Tom Joad's final speech in *Grapes of Wrath*, but there is obviously a lot of Steinbeck in it. And as Library of Congress film historian David Parker says, "Ninety years from now, people are still going to be choked up when they hear Fonda say those words again. And that's no small thing."

What Tom Joad said to his mother when she asked what would become of him was, "Well, maybe it's like Casey says: A fella ain't got a soul of his own, just a little piece of a big soul, the one big soul that belongs to everybody. And then, it don't matter; I'll be around. In the dark. I'll be everywhere. Wherever you can look. Wherever there's a fight, so hungry people can eat, I'll be there. Whenever there's a cop beatin' up a guy, I'll be there. I'll be in the way guys yell when they're mad, and I'll be in the way kids laugh when they're hungry and they know supper's ready. And when people are eatin' stuff they raise, and livin' in the house they build, I'll be there, too."

MA JOAD: "I don't understand it, Tom."

TOM: "Me neither, Ma. It's just somethin' I've been thinkin' about. Give me your hand.

"Goodbye."

Television will probably never be as good as it was when you could turn it on and see what Dave Garroway was up to.

"Well, here we are," Dave Garroway said, materializing on-camera in bow tie and glasses and an enormous yoke of a lavalier mike—instantly indelible trademarks—for the premiere of the *Today* show forty years ago. "And good morning to you—the very first good morning of what I hope and suspect will be a great many good mornings between you and me. Here it is . . . January 14, 1952, when NBC begins a new program called *Today* and—if it doesn't sound too revolutionary—I really believe begins a new kind of television."

We usually don't think of television personalities in the large-scale terms reserved for movie stars, or political notables, or illustrious artists of one more rarefied realm or another—in terms of "greatness." But what Dave Garroway did on, and for, television, was great, on *Today* and *Wide Wide World* and *Garroway at Large*. It was clear and direct and intimate and real.

Dave Garroway was very important to television. If this were theater we were talking about, his death would be like all the Barrymores going at once; nearly everyone who's come after him has owed him something. He wasn't just the born "communicator"—the title originally given him as *Today* host—he was an inventor. Inventing TV-the-machine was not that hard. Dave Garroway helped invent what you put on it once you've got it.

And because he used television so well, Dave Garroway became very important to the people who met him through it. He knew the secret of television. He knew how to be the perfect guest in millions of homes at once. Before it was all over, he was family. A few years ago, Dave Garroway and Lee Lawrence, one of the early *Today* producers and Garroway's close friend, were walking down Madison Avenue when a stranger rushed up and said, "Say, David, there's something I've been wanting to ask you for a long time," as if they were old pals. Neither Garroway nor Lawrence had ever seen the man before.

Utterly at home in front of a camera, able to look into its lens and talk amiably with everyone with whom he made this new kind of twentieth-century contact, Garroway was in private a shy man, a putterer, a jazz buff, and, for all of his life, a scholar, an inquisitor. He could never learn enough. What made him so good on television was that he thought television should be a continuing education, for him and for the people who watched.

Yet he never played the professor. He was a fellow student, damn smart, but no show-off. He was so eager and so readily fascinated that he drew you into any discussion, whether the subject was the fate of the earth or National Donut Week. He brought to the *Today* show his old theme song (circa 1949),

Larry Elgart's recording of "Sentimental Journey," and a brilliantly simple way of saying good-bye; his right arm raised and his hand open flat and the word "peace," spoken long before it had been politicized and buzzed up.

On the thirtieth-anniversary edition of the *Today* show, Jane Pauley asked Garroway why he was so averse to "stuffy" things. Still wearing glasses—thicker now—and with white hair swept back and sticking over his collar, Wizard-of-Oz style, Garroway told her, "I don't like stuffy things or people very much, I guess. There was so much to talk about and do, and there still is in this world, that I don't find it a very stuffy world even today."

Five years earlier, Garroway also showed up for the twenty-fifth anniversary of the *Today* show. While historian Daniel Boorstin was being interviewed on camera by someone else, members of the show's cast talked among themselves, or primped, or yawned. But there was Garroway, standing in the wings, watching a monitor and hanging on every one of Boorstin's words. How lucky are the people who can sustain that kind of passion for experience. These are the kind of people who ought to be on television.

In 1975, Garroway sat down for a long interview about TV's early days, in which he played so enormous a role. There was a sadness haunting the reminiscence, though, because Garroway hadn't been working. "There haven't been any offers," he said. He had just returned from the Soviet Union, where he got to look through the world's biggest telescope. Astronomy was a lifelong hobby. After the death of his first wife in 1961, Garroway left *Today,* and the following summer was observed by friends staying up all night to stare silently at the Milky Way through a telescope at his place in Aspen.

But when recalling the first morning of *Today,* Garroway was affable and animated. "I remember it as though it were now," he said. "I mean, I don't remember exactly what and who were on the show, but I remember the great feel of it. I was delighted with it. I felt pleased with myself as I perhaps never have before or since. And when it was all over, the whole crew applauded. It was the best sound I ever heard."

Garroway strolled into untested waters and showed everybody else how to navigate. He was virtually never at a loss and never uncomfortable on-camera. For author Max Wilk's book *The Golden Age of Television*, Mort Werner, the original producer of *Today*, recalled why he had picked Garroway for the show even though he didn't think, at first, that he was the right man for the job. Garroway called him from Chicago and asked him to fly in for dinner—a meal, it turned out, of baked beans and root beer at Garroway's apartment.

"We ate," Werner recalled, "and then we sat and talked all night and I discovered a lot of things about Dave. First, that he was very well educated; second, that he had worked for NBC radio for many years in several different cities as a newscaster and a reporter; and finally, that he'd won the Chicago Open golf tournament, which wasn't pertinent. But I really fell in love with the man on a one-to-one basis. So I came back to New York and I said, 'I've found my host—Dave Garroway.' "

For *Wide Wide World*, a Sunday afternoon NBC program that celebrated TV's ability to obliterate distances, Garroway would sit on a stool and play national interlocutor. Cameras were mounted in roller coasters or attached to men parachuting from planes. You saw old railroad engines and a real western roundup and the Grand Canyon.

And Garroway. He was the calm center that somehow kept you riveted. Part of his talent with the camera was instinctual, part of it was brilliantly devised—and part of it may have grown out of a kind of alienation.

"It was the funniest thing about looking into that camera," he explained. "I didn't have any idea what it would be like that first time. But when we got on the air, I felt very warm and comfortable—strangely so—instead of being frightened. The lens seemed to be so direct and friendly, really, almost as if I could see somebody there. It was a black channel to the people, a neutron star. I still think that way. It stuck with me all my life. I am much more comfortable and more in communication with whoever is at the end of that black hole than I am with someone in person."

The word "peace" got trampled during the sixties, so Dave Garroway—years before Dan Rather briefly tried using it— changed his farewell to "courage," because he said he'd read a poem written by Amelia Earhart before her last flight, "and the last lines of it were, 'Courage is the price which life exacts for granting peace,' " he said. "Up to then, I'd been supplicating— 'Please give me peace.' This was a way in order to find it."

Garroway had a knack for haunting sign-offs. He would close *Wide Wide World* with a few lines from Edna St. Vincent Millay: "The world stands out on either side, /No wider than the heart is wide; /Above the world is stretched the sky, /No higher than the soul is high."

Peace.

F I R E   I N   T H E   B E L L Y

~~~~~~
~~~~~~

With the possible exception of his own death, Paddy Chayefsky never took anything lying down.

That at least was the public perception of his life and work; that he was a maverick, irascible iconoclast. He lit one little candle, and then he cursed the darkness anyway.

His first fat fame as a writer came with the gentle and beautifully crafted play *Marty*, written for television in 1953. It was a landmark in the history of the medium. It was a landmark in the history of landmarks. The plight of a lonely butcher became, for that hour on the air (and later as a movie), a crisis of earthshaking magnitude.

But Chayefsky's later successes, the ones through which contemporary audiences knew him best, were boisterous and ferocious social comedies, *The Hospital* and *Network,* both about microcosmic cultures in advanced stages of nervous breakdown. And Chayefsky's image as an angry middle-aged man was bolstered in front of millions of TV viewers when, at the 1978 Academy Awards ceremonies, he rebuked actress Vanessa Redgrave for using her Oscar acceptance speech as a platform for anti-Zionist propaganda earlier in the evening.

To be appropriately overblown about it, Paddy Chayefsky remained a passionate man no matter how increasingly passionless the age. Many may have thought of him, and he may have thought of himself, as a lone voice on a soapbox, a man who might have been a street-corner philosopher if he hadn't been blessed with a gift for fervent dramaturgy.

He mobilized words and marched them off to war, and sometimes went to war to defend them. When he didn't like what director Ken Russell did to his script for the film *Altered States,* he disowned the movie and had his real name, Sidney Aaron, posted in the credits.

Both his own personal, all-purpose indignation and his prowess at recognizing marketable sentiments were summed up in the catchphrase that his *Network* contributed to American life in the frustrating seventies: "I'm mad as hell, and I'm not going to take it anymore!" In the movie, citizens run to their windows and scream it into the night. It was a cry worthy of the Boston Tea Party or abolition or the Vietnam War.

It was the capper to a magnificent career of rants and raves and sound and fury.

Chayefsky had been one of the architects of the golden age of live television drama. He and other New York writers saw television as enticingly virgin territory, a place to perfect skills, the niftiest workshop ever conceived. But more than that, television offered awesome possibilities for a new and truly national theater—piercingly intimate as a stage, yet with access to the widest audience ever known.

He recalled later that the rewards were almost entirely creative. "We were all broke, and we worked for nothing." For the original script to *Marty*, he was paid a pauperly nine hundred dollars. It was a kitchen-sink drama in more ways than one.

Marty's leap into the mass consciousness was immediate and lasting. People picked up on the sparse realism of its dialogue, on its authentic cryptic poetry. To this day, a casual conversation between two people about plans for the evening might include a paraphrase of Paddy Chayefsky: "Whaddayou wanna do tonight?" "I don't know, Marty; whaddayou wanna do?"

The networks and Hollywood killed live drama as the fifties ended. Led by the lamentable example of ABC and Warner Bros., and Walt Disney, CBS and NBC also decided it would be cheaper and less hassle to fill prime time with filmed programming plunked out on assembly lines in Los Angeles. The new national theater became just another rundown movie house.

But it was magical there for a while, when Rod Serling and Reginald Rose and William Gibson and Paddy Chayefsky reigned supreme. They might have felt a little—all right, just a little, but more than not at all—like Shakespeare writing for the Globe.

No Paddy Chayefsky play or movie was complete without a Great Speech, usually delivered fortissimo, often the barely filtered voice of the author. In *Network*, the big bow-wow went to William Holden, who, as a fired network news president, accuses Fay Dunaway, as his successor—also his mistress—of having made the ultimate sellout:

"You are television incarnate, Diana—indifferent to suffering, insensitive to joy. All of life is reduced to the common rubble of banality. War, murder, death, are all the same to you as bottles of beer. The daily business of life is a corrupt comedy. You even shatter the sensations of time and space into jagged fragments of minutes, split-seconds and instant replays. You are madness, Diana, virulent madness, and whatever you touch dies with you."

Although he was hurt that some of the people he knew in broadcasting took the lambasting personally, Chayefsky said later he had no regrets about voicing such rancorous opinions. "I meant every word of it," he said. "I watch television and I become numb."

One month before the release of *Network*, I phoned Paddy Chayefsky at his office in Manhattan. He was listed in the phone book, and he answered the phone himself. I asked him for an interview; he said he would rather not give one. We talked for half an hour. His reason for not wanting to work in television again was simple, he said: "I don't want to be hysterical all the time."

Paddy Chayefsky was the embodiment of what people mean when they say, "He puts his heart into his work." His heart, yes—and his spleen, and pieces of his soul. His carping was music, and his anger joyful noise.

WILDCAT

〜〜〜〜〜〜〜〜〜〜〜〜〜〜〜〜〜〜〜〜〜〜〜〜〜〜〜〜

S tomper of grapes, wrapper of chocolates, bottler of salad dressing, stealer of footprints, aspiring saxophonist, would-be chorus girl, wife, mother, friend, neighbor, and one-time pitchperson for an 80-proof health tonic, she set her putty nose on fire and dipped it in coffee to extinguish the blaze, wrapped a thirty-pound cheese as a baby so she could smuggle it onto a transatlantic flight, and put so much yeast into the bread she was baking that the mutant loaf slid out of the oven and pinned her against the kitchen sink.

Lucille Ball is gone, but Lucy Ricardo remains behind, still hatching plots and mending fences and trying to break into show business. Because of her, Lucille Ball deserves the title of Television's Biggest Star, its female Chaplin. When Ball persuaded CBS to air the *I Love Lucy* pilot she'd made with her husband Desi Arnaz in 1951, television had just gotten its foot in the American door. Now it would never leave.

Nor would Lucy.

Marital sitcoms preceded and followed *I Love Lucy;* none were so consistently funny. They may have had an "I" and they may have had a "Love" but they didn't have a Lucy. It helped, of course, that Lucy and Desi were married in real life, just as on the show. "Lucy Goes to the Hospital," the highest-rated episode of the series, aired on the night that Lucille Ball gave birth to Desi Arnaz, Jr. Forty-four million people tuned in, it has often been pointed out, whereas only twenty million watched the inauguration of Dwight D. Eisenhower the next day.

"They liked Ike," said Walter Matthau at the 1976 Kennedy Center Honors, "but they loved Lucy." Arnaz, too ill to attend, sent remarks to be read in his name, including the observation, " 'I Love Lucy' was never just a title." Loving Lucy seemed something that was unanimous, universal, uncontested. It was common ground, an American passion to rival baseball and hot dogs and an American export to rival jazz and blue jeans. They might as well have added it to the Pledge of Allegiance: "one nation, under God, indivisible, with liberty and Lucy for all."

When, in 1989, Lucy went to the hospital for real, it was for major heart surgery, and people everywhere reacted with the kind of anxious concern usually reserved for close relations or friends one knows personally. They felt they knew Lucy personally. She was family. This has to do with the nature of television. And with the nature of Lucy.

"It's a wild medium, television," Lucy had said in an interview. "The closeness, which was apparent from the first two years that we were on the air, was, at the time, a great surprise, because we had no idea that people would run up and want to touch you. They had never done that before. But they felt so close to you, because you had been in their living rooms. Now, of course, it's old hat; everybody knows it. It's the quickest form of recognition in the world."

When *I Love Lucy* is recalled in tributes, it's usually the slapsticky clips that show up—the grapes, the bread, Lucy dipped into a vat of starch, Lucy dressed up as Superman and shooing pigeons off a window ledge, Lucy toppling over from the weight of a huge headdress in a Hollywood production number.

But plenty of performers were doing slapstick on TV in the early fifties. Martin and Lewis rarely finished a show without demolishing the studio. Abbott and Costello re-created their rowdy vaudeville routines. Milton Berle wielded pies and powder puffs and flounced around in gowns. What Lucy did was to domesticate slapstick, to make it plausible within a narrative framework, to make it a logical extension for a patently and endearingly zany characterization. She put it in context, and the audience enjoyed believing that someone really could go through life romping from one wacky antic to another.

She was also able to do physical comedy without sacrificing femininity, a trick that some of her more raucous contemporaries were unable to master. There was simple facial slapstick, too: an array of broad expressions to register fear or delight or cunning. She perfected a grimace of dread that the scriptwriters referred to as "the spider," because it looks like somebody spying a spider and going "Ugggh."

Slapstick was only part of the show's appeal, anyway, and only one aspect of the Lucy character, which viewers saw as veritably defining irrepressible. Lucy is pluck and vitality incarnate, and these were states of being that Ball was particularly well qualified to convey.

Like most long-running hits, *Lucy* depended also on fortuitous alchemy. Lucky and Ricky and their landlords and friends Fred and Ethel Mertz seemed a deliciously quixotic quartet, unlikely yet ideal. They were not unlike the Kramdens and the Nortons of the harsher, less farcical *The Honeymooners*—not unlike the four fanciful wayfarers of *The Wizard of Oz*, either.

A posterized still from *I Love Lucy* shows the stars in a convertible crossing the George Washington Bridge on their way to Hollywood, singing "California, Here I Come." It's a comedy Mount Rushmore.

The Lucy-Ethel relationship was as important to the show as the Lucy-Ricky relationship. Time and again Lucy drafted Ethel into madcap schemes and conspiracies designed to foil repressive husbands. They were the first and best example of female bonding in television. Though they might argue bitterly over the presidency of the Wednesday Afternoon Fine Arts League, or spat because both showed up wearing the same new dress, by the end of the show the rift was *phfft*—they were friends again. As a finale one week, they sang Cole Porter's "Friendship," the song that had also ended Lucy's MGM musical *DuBarry Was a Lady* in 1943.

Beneath the slapstick and gag lines, *I Love Lucy* had its own kind of truth and tenderness. For those who remember Monday nights built around it in the fifties during its first run, or those who know it from the endlessly repeated reruns—179 episodes— now in syndication, *I Love Lucy* is not just watched but warmly embraced. And it warmly embraces back.

Lucille Ball made seventy films. In *Best Foot Forward*, she played herself. But few of the movies were memorable, or even good. In 1940 she starred in *Too Many Girls*, the belabored movie version of the Rodgers and Hart Broadway hit. She sang "I Didn't Know What Time It Was" with somebody's else's synched-in voice. What makes the film notable is that Arnaz was also in the cast; the two of them met during production.

After *I Love Lucy*, there were Lucy-Desi specials that lacked the spontaneity of the weekly series. Ball and Arnaz divorced. Lucy appeared in subsequent series like *Here's Lucy* and *The Lucy Show*, but the old chemistry was missing. In 1985 she played a straight dramatic role, Flora the bag lady, in a CBS movie, *The Stone Pillow*. In the opening scene she awakes on the street under a blanket of trash bags and says, "Well, I'm still here."

Then in 1986 Ball made an abortive attempt at a comedy comeback, *Life with Lucy*, on ABC. A few weeks before the premiere she sat in her suite on the studio lot in Hollywood and talked about her reasons for returning to work—mainly that she was bored and couldn't busy herself sufficiently with "shopping." In person, she was not the sweetest little thing. She was known offscreen as a tough, demanding dynamo. Appropriately enough, her Broadway hit *Wildcat* had her singing a brassily assertive "Hey, Look Me Over." And she looked even older than her seventy-five years. She had eyebrow pencil where there were no eyebrows and pink lipstick, which she continually blotted with a napkin, where there were no lips.

She had brought a homemade meatloaf sandwich to the studio for lunch. In the bathroom was a bottle of henna rinse, the potion that first turned her into a redhead in the forties and kept her one from then on. During the McCarthy hysteria of the fifties, her hair was interpreted as evidence of Communist leanings. Right-wing nuts put her on their "Red Channels" blacklist because, it was discovered, her grandfather had once voted Communist in an election in the thirties. Lucy explained he was an eccentric, and was permitted to continue with her career.

Like everybody else, Ball said, she too watched *I Love Lucy* reruns. A Los Angeles station routinely ran two of them a day, and more on weekends. "I don't like some of the shows that I look at," she said. "Some of the old *I Love Lucy*s are silly. Some of the old *I Love Lucy*s, when we were just starting out, grate me a little. Do I laugh at them? Sometimes. I study them and enjoy them and I wish I'd done it differently lots of times—most of the time—but very few I really laugh at. I find that now I usually spend my time looking at Viv. Viv was sensational. I enjoy every move Viv made. She was something."

She was asked about a trademark of the show that emerged from the studio audience—a woman's voice saying a loud "Aw-oh" at points in the plot when one of Lucy's schemes was about to backfire. On almost all of the shows, there was no canned laughter or the kind of augmentation now called "sweetening." Ball said she didn't know who the "Aw-oh" lady was, but she said it might have been her mother. Watching the reruns, Ball said, she could sometimes hear her mother's laughter coming up from the bleachers, louder than anyone else's.

Lucy made no attempt to be funny or tell funny stories during the interview, though her husband, Gary Morton, whom she married after divorcing Arnaz, made her laugh a few times. He coaxed her into doing her impression of Vincente Minnelli, who directed the Arnazes in *The Long Long Trailer,* a so-so movie made when they were blooming national darlings. The impression consisted of Lucy waving her hands furiously in front of her face and saying in a prissy voice, "Everybody go crazy! Everybody go crazy!"

Interviewed years earlier as she prepared a CBS special, Ball said she had no intention of writing an autobiography. "There've been unauthorized books written about me that I've never commented on. But I wouldn't even want to write a book. No. You really don't tell the truth until you're about eighty-five and I don't expect to be around that long. I don't want to be."

Recovering in Cedars-Sinai Medical Center from surgery, Ball had the luxury of, in essence, reading her own obits. Tributes and accolades poured forth, and thousands of letters wishing her well arrived at the hospital. If she looked out her window, she might have seen a large banner posted on the Hard Rock Cafe across the street: HARD ROCK LOVES LUCY. On the day she died, a caller asked a young woman at the café how long the sign would stay up. Not knowing Ball was gone, she said, "Until she's feeling better." Told the bad news, she became too emotional to continue talking.

Later that day the sign was changed to GOD BLESS LUCY.

"My wife—that's the very lovely redhead over there," Ricky said of Lucy on a show marking the Ricardos' fifteenth wedding anniversary. They celebrate that anniversary over and over as the episodes are recycled and its time comes up again. Some people know the dialogue before the actors speak it, and they sing along when Ricky serenades Lucy at a party with "The Anniversary Waltz," accompanied by a platoon of strolling violins.

For audiences watching in late 1955, when that episode first aired, the Ricardos epitomized marital bliss. For those who watch today, it's bliss, period. *I Love Lucy* was never just a title.

H

e was most famous for whom he loved.
Lucy.
But Desi Arnaz was important in his own right—a
risk-taker and innovator whose influence on television
extends beyond the phenomenal success and longevity of *I Love Lucy*, in which he costarred and for
which he served as executive producer. Still in reruns throughout
the world decades after it ceased production, some U.S. stations
run two or more episodes a day.

"Some people called it superficial, with no literary or intellectual values, only escapism," Arnaz wrote in *A Book*, his unas-
sumingly titled 1976 autobiography. "Okay, but I see nothing
wrong with a show that is just that." Lucille Ball and Desi Arnaz,
marriage partners and business partners throughout the fifties,
helped define the decade for Americans and helped determine
the course of television for years and years to come.

"The success of 'I Love Lucy' is something that only happens once in a lifetime, if you are fortunate enough to have it happen at all," Arnaz wrote. "As for Lucy herself, all I can say is that I loved her very much, and in my own and perhaps peculiar way, I will always love her."

Sweet. By published accounts, the marriage was rocky when it wasn't stormy. Arnaz was said to be compulsively unfaithful. But during the Eisenhower years, the public saw a mercifully rosy picture, the former MGM glamour girl and the raven-haired Cuban bandleader who met at RKO in 1940. Sixteen years later they bought the studio for themselves, renaming it Desilu.

Under Arnaz's supervision, Desilu turned out hits like *The Untouchables, Our Miss Brooks,* and *December Bride.* From the anthology series *Desilu Playhouse* came the pilots for *Mission: Impossible* and *The Twilight Zone.* But the cornerstone of the company, as Mickey Mouse was to Walt Disney, remained *I Love Lucy.*

Originally CBS Chairman William S. Paley didn't want Arnaz to be part of the package. It was Ball who insisted her real husband play her husband on the show. Arnaz earned the respect of CBS when, while going over budgets for the second season, he discovered the network had mistakenly allocated $1 million too much. No one else had noticed the error. Things like that can really endear you to a network.

"That changed CBS's opinion of him," says Bart Andrews, author of *The I Love Lucy Book.* It is, Andrews says, a mistake to remember Arnaz as "a second-rate actor in a hit show, or as Mr. Lucille Ball. In fact, he was much more than that. He was a real pioneer in television, and he helped make the medium what it is today."

With cinematographer Karl Freund, who'd shot Lucy in *Dubarry Was a Lady* when both were at MGM, Arnaz invented the so-called three-camera technique used on most TV sitcoms today. The network had wanted *Lucy* to be live, but by insisting it be filmed, Arnaz saw to it the show would endure as well as prosper. Using three cameras made it possible to film the show before a studio audience and record the sounds of real laughter. The technique has been adopted for videotape on such latter-day hits as *The Golden Girls* and *The Cosby Show.*

"Desi was doing three jobs and doing them magnificently," Ball recalled years later, "and I marvel now when I think back." Gary Morton, successor to Arnaz as Ball's husband, said, "It's amazing what this man did. I look at that ingenuity there—it's fantastic."

Arnaz developed skills as a comic actor, and even played the rare serious scene. His longest time on screen without Lucy, about five minutes, occurs in a 1954 episode called "Ricky Minds the Baby," in which he touchingly recites "Little Red Riding Hood" in Spanish to his infant son.

The series was an enormous and virtually instant hit. To say that Lucy was the whole show underestimates the peculiar alchemy that made it work. On the air, Arnaz was an uncommonly colorful foil, and his fracturing of the English language proved a durable source of humor. He said "dunt" instead of "don't," "wunt" instead of "won't" and "thin" instead of "thing," and told Lucy she was good at "snikky swishes," which meant "sneaky switches." She bounced her antics off his big pop eyes, and he regularly exploded with kinetic alarm. A longtime song-and-dance man, he performed numbers like "Babalu" (his trademark conga-thumper), "I'll See You in C-u-b-a" and other pop hits from, or about, his native island. Lucy referred to him as her "hot-blooded Cuban."

Backstage, Arnaz later admitted, all was not harmonious cheer. William Frawley and Vivian Vance, who played neighbors and landlords Fred and Ethel Mertz, detested one another. Frawley, according to Arnaz, referred to Vance with terms like "bitch," "silly broad," and "fat-ass." Vance told associates no one would believe she could be married to "that old goat," which sounds like a line from the show. The story goes that Vance's contract required her to stay twenty pounds overweight so as to make Lucy look better.

The story also goes that Mr. and Mrs. Arnaz once had a raucous spat while staying at the Château Marmont Hotel in Hollywood, where years later John Belushi died, and that in the course of it, a suitcase full of money spilled open, pouring currency down on Sunset Boulevard from a balcony. Stories do go. On the air, however, none of the backstage hostilities showed. It was a love story America loved, and wanted to believe. One week, Desi crooned lyrics to the title tune into his wife's ear: "I love Lucy and she loves me, we're as happy as two can be. Sometimes we quarrel but then, how we love making up again."

With all its slapsticky highjinks, *Lucy* was grounded in a kind of reality, a wistful and wishful vision of middle-class domestic bliss.

Lucy earned a 71.8 Nielsen rating and a 92 share, meaning nearly three-quarters of the TV sets in America were tuned to CBS to see it. For the 1952–53 season, *I Love Lucy* averaged a 67.9 rating, more than all three networks combined normally get today, and the highest for any series episode ever. By comparison, ratings for *Cosby*, the biggest sitcom hit of the eighties, averaged a 34.3 in the 1985–86 season, its most successful.

There were 11 million TV households in the United States when *Lucy* premiered in 1951, and 45 million when it signed off a decade later. Everything had changed. And yet *I Love Lucy* would never be off the air.

For the Arnazes, it was not just a show but the foundation of an empire. At Desi's insistence, the couple agreed to work for $4,000 a week instead of $5,000 the first season provided they could own the shows outright. In 1957, CBS bought back those rights from Desi and Lucy for a lousy $5 million—but that was a lot of money then.

Andrews interviewed Arnaz for his book eight times from 1975 to 1977. "He was not jolly at all," Andrews recalls. "Neither was Lucy. These were pretty serious people. He was very sentimental though. Whenever we got into a heavy subject about *I Love Lucy*, he was sort of crying. He broke down a few times and had to leave the room when we talked about Lucy, who I think he still loved to this day."

In 1976, Arnaz appeared with son Desi, Jr., on an episode of *Saturday Night Live*. Several sketches lampooned *I Love Lucy*, but affectionately; one crossbred the sitcom with Desilu's crime series *The Untouchables*. Desi's raven hair was dove-white now, but he looked both roguish and distinguished under it. He proved he could still thump a conga drum with the best of them, although of course most of the best of them were long gone.

In his last years, he was ill and, some said, lonely. He said he would have attended a 1986 Kennedy Center gala at which his wife was honored, but poor health kept him away. His doctor said he smoked too many Cuban cigars.

Trying to analyze the incomparably lasting appeal of the program he helped create, Arnaz wrote, "I am sure there have been occasions when you had a great time at a party for no particular reason. Why did you? The chemistry, the mixture of the people there, made it fun." So it was with *I Love Lucy*. Though the host has left, the party goes on. Perhaps forever.

Who Lucy loved will be remembered, too.

ilda Radner thought she wasn't beautiful. She was wrong about that.

A TV picture is made of light, and Gilda Radner supplemented that light with a quirky glow of her own. She did it by just being herself, but also by playing a gallery of endearing eccentrics on *Saturday Night Live:* the half-deaf fussbudget Emily Litella ("What's all this about Soviet jewelry?"), the blabbily oblivious Baba Wawa, the postnasal Lisa Loopner, and Roseanne Roseannadanna, a whacked-out frizzoid whose recollections of excruciating gross-outs would always include the interjection "I thought I was gonna die."

In May of 1989, in Los Angeles, at forty-two, Gilda Radner did. That night, hosting the last program of *Saturday Night Live*'s fourteenth season, comedian Steve Martin introduced a brief tape that showed Gilda at her impish best, romping with Martin through an affectionate spoof of romantic movie-musical numbers to the strains of "Dancing in the Dark."

As a preface to the clip, Martin, choking back tears, said, "You know, I've been coming here to do *Saturday Night Live* since 1976, and the thing that brings you back to the show is the people you get to work with. And I'd like to show you something we recorded on this stage in 1978."

In the number, Gilda and Steve, both dressed in white, chase each other around the studio, two strangers having a daft chance encounter, all swoons and swoops and pirouettes. Afterward, quieting an ovation from the studio audience, Martin said, "When I look at this tape, I can't help but think how great she was, and how young I looked. Gilda, we miss you."

Gilda Radner was an honor student in the show's first graduating class, on its "Not Ready for Prime Time Players" when it premiered on NBC in 1975. The program proceeded to reshape and reorder television comedy, delivering it into the hands of an irreverent upstart generation that had grown up tethered to the tube and knew all its dirty little secrets. The impression Gilda and her classmates made on the national consciousness has proven indelible; they are regarded now as pioneers, tough riders and musketeers. They were party crashers who put on a better party than the one they crashed.

Gilda was the cutest, the sweetest, the most adorable. Beneath the wonderful characters was a wonderful her. She also appeared, as the years went by, to be the *SNL* alum least adversely affected by instant fans and its hazards. She always seemed to have her feet on the ground and to keep a jaundiced, self-mocking attitude. That probably served her well when she developed ovarian cancer and underwent seventeen months of treatment, including chemotherapy. Returning to the public eye in 1988 after a two-year absence, she bounced through an antic edition of *It's Garry Shandling's Show* on cable TV.

"I haven't been on television for a while," Gilda says on her first appearance. "Oh that . . . yeah, what was wrong?" Shandling asks her. "Oh, I had cancer," Gilda says matter-of-factly, adding, "What did you have?"

Throughout the show, she would upstage Shandling by raising her arms in a victory sign that inevitably prompted audience cheers. Shandling would catch her looking directly into the camera, the technique that only he was supposed to use. "I'll bop you," he threatened. A falling coconut did bop her, right on the head, later in the show.

At about the time she taped the program, she began work on a book about her experience with cancer, *It's Always Something*, another of the catchphrases favored by the redoubtable Ms. Roseannadanna. She became a familiar, cheering figure at The Wellness Community in Santa Monica, where she offered counsel and support to others with life-threatening diseases.

"We all would like somebody to say, 'Everything for sure is okay,' " she said of her remission. "That's like saying that for sure if I go back on TV, it's going to be a success. You can't. You just go on with your life. There's an unknown, yeah, but there's an unknown in everybody's life. Cancer is just more up-front. You forge ahead."

She had left *Saturday Night Live* with some regrets, but the timing felt right. "*Saturday Night* made us all famous, and there was no way to retrieve the underdog image we once had," she noted a few months later. "As we all went out into the world to make movies or whatever, then suddenly the less people there were to make fun of, because they're your peers."

Nevertheless, she was grateful to have attended the comedy college of the air. "I think our television show was incredible. It was theater at this heightened sense, theater being immediately documented and captured. It was this amazing life that was like a dog's life, 'cause there were seven years in every one year. Really! Truly! It got hard for the rest of life to compare with that kind of energy and the feeling of celebration once you got through it."

Some people expected that Gilda would remain in television, becoming a Lucille Ball for the eighties. She enjoyed physical comedy. "I'd like to do a show where coconuts hit me on the head," she said after taping *Shandling*. A few times on *SNL*, she played a Lucy-like character. Once she was the wacky redhead on a factory assembly line, but instead of chocolate candies passing by on a conveyor belt, there were nuclear warheads. She dropped one and it blew up. "Waaaaaa!"

Instead of staying in TV, Gilda took her act to other stages, among them the Winter Garden Theater in New York, where her delightful one-woman revue kept having its run extended. Eventually Mike Nichols filmed it as *Gilda Live*. She played many of the characters from *SNL*, including Loopner, whose tortured rendering of "The Way We Were" on the piano reduced her to blubbering tears.

After *Saturday Night Live*, Chevy Chase went on to make execrable movies, Dan Aykroyd made good ones and bad ones, John Belushi died of a drug overdose, Laraine Newman and Garrett Morris largely disappeared from view, Bill Murray became a film superstar, and Jane Curtin costarred on *Kate and Allie*, a prime-time sitcom on CBS. Gilda was more adventurous than any of them, really. In addition to *Gilda Live*, she appeared in Jean Kerr's stage play *Lunch Hour*. She made movies with her second husband, Gene Wilder, but except for *The Lady in Red*, they were not successful, and Gilda said she was "never comfortable" with the movie camera.

Still, one had every reason to anticipate that many more nights and years ahead would be made happier and funnier because Gilda Radner would keep popping up in them.

Through all her appearances, she remained to some recognizable degree the little girl from Detroit who realized at the age of ten that her wits and not her looks would be her greatest resource. Journalist Marion Clark, encountering Gilda during her meteoric ascent in 1976, saw in her not only a blithely talented comic actress, but also a kindred spirit—a young woman who knew the pain of the occasional dateless Friday night and who maintained not-so-secret passions for cigarettes and pastries. She still used words like *ookie.*

"She's the pretty, smart, funny and most of all nice girl you still are," Marion Clark wrote, addressing herself. "She didn't make the cheerleading team, either, but she did the prom decorations and she made all her own clothes and all the girls liked her and tried to fix her up with dates."

Gilda told Clark about a blind date who arrived to pick her up one night and, taking a long look at her, "said to me right out, 'You realize I can't take you out, don't you?' Well, I realized it then." Another boy canceled a date by telling her that he had mononucleosis "and that he was going to have it for the rest of his life."

Oh but the funny girls are still the most fun.

They're the ones you remember and smile.

In 1980, preparing for *Lunch Hour,* Gilda was full of life and full of possibilities. Cancer had not been diagnosed. "I feel like somebody's been so generous with experiences for me," she said then. "Whosoever is controlling it, I mean. I've had a real generosity there, so sometimes I think maybe I'm getting this all now, and quickly, 'cause there's not going to be a whole lot later.

"I mean, maybe I'm gonna die or something. I know that's

an awful way to think, but I have been real fortunate. Real lucky." With that, she jumped up and grabbed her lumpy purse and danced to the center of the rehearsal hall. Literally danced—skipping, prancing, larking. Sunlight streamed through the second-story windows, but it couldn't hold a candle to her.

S A M U R A I   C O M I C

guess I want *everything*," John Belushi once said. But lives lived to excess, lives devoted to it, sometimes end early. John Belushi's ended when he was thirty-three, and by most accounts his appetites were still defiantly enormous. He was not easily appeased. Those who came in contact with him, through television or in person or both, will not have hazy memories. The memories will always roar. He could not be casually encountered and will not be casually forgotten.

He was a riot.

On NBC's *Saturday Night Live*, where Belushi was a founding member of the original company of players and writers, he tore into roles that often depended on physical and emotional extremes: the easily antagonized, oddly plump samurai swordsman who might be found checking in guests at a motel or doing strenuous flips at a disco or running a delicatessen—anywhere you would never find a samurai swordsman; the boisterous proprietor of a noisy Greek diner, where he chanted "chee-boogie, chee-boogie" and the deflating, "No Coke, Pepsi"; or as the ultimate in angry young men, delivering news commentaries that degenerated into frenzies, Belushi twirling himself into a fury, spinning in his chair, flailing his arms in the air, then disappearing in a cloud of pique behind the desk.

Film critic Gary Arnold, reviewing Belushi's feature debut in *Animal House,* described his portrayal of Bluto, unrepentant campus slob, as "an amalgam of unchecked appetites in vaguely human form." When the movie was sneak-previewed, youthful audiences applauded when the name John Belushi came on the screen in the opening credits. People were crazy about this nut. He was John the Liberator to them.

Animal House became the highest-grossing comedy in movie history up to that time, eventually to be surpassed by *Ghostbusters*, which featured Belushi's friend and fellow Blues Brother Dan Aykroyd. A part for Belushi had been written in the script, but he was gone by then. In a way, though, he did appear. The figure of a blobbish, sybaritic spook that materialized several times during the movie, once raiding a room-service cart, and did a final fly-by before the closing credits, seemed to represent the departed spirit of the great class clown.

Offscreen, Belushi was known as a strenuous and nearly tireless partier, particularly during his five years on *Saturday Night Live*. Following the completion of one more-or-less-official cast party after the show, Belushi and Aykroyd and pals would retire with invited guests to their own scuzzy excuse for an after-hours haunt, where liquor and, alas, harder drugs flowed until the sun came up.

In those days, you could do drugs and have sex and not worry that you might wake up dead. Except that one morning, John Belushi did.

Belushi had something besides a wild side. He could turn meek and sheepish, for instance, when presented with a compliment on his work. He'd lower his eyes and smile incredulously and ask, "Really? Did you really like it?" It was as if he'd been handed a puppy on Christmas morning.

In 1975, high on the first gush of success for *Saturday Night Live,* Belushi came to Washington with Aykroyd, Chevy Chase, and Lorne Michaels, who produced and essentially created the show.

They rode from monument to monument in a limousine that day, Belushi posing playfully for photos with a startled Park Ranger at the Lincoln Memorial. In Georgetown, John decided he wanted a drink and asked if it were legal to carry open liquor on the streets. It wasn't. He disappeared into a liquor store and emerged with, of all things, a bottle of Lancer's. It was wrapped in a paper bag. Everybody took a drink out of it and then ran across the street to Martin's Bar, where they had lunch. Aykroyd barely missed getting run over by a No. 34 bus.

Chase was cold and snobbish, already imagining himself the big star of the show. Belushi was warm and friendly, and it mattered to him that he made you laugh—for free, for nothing, because it was something he had to do. On the Mall, he picked up a long stick off the ground and made it a cane; he became a cantankerous old politician, hobbling along by the reflecting pool, while Aykroyd, immediately picking up the cue, took the part of a hustling reporter, calling out, "Senator, Senator, please, Senator," only to be brushed away by Belushi, who would stop for a moment and then resume hobbling. They chased each other into the distance this way.

Chase stood there looking baffled. But his then-girlfriend, joining in the laughter, paused to say, "Such children!"

Precisely. Such children.

They were the children of television, too, the first real members of the TV generation to seize control of it for themselves. The attitude was one of elation mixed with disdain; "Prime time sucks," was what Belushi liked to say. But here in late night, they could somehow corrupt television in their own clever way without being co-opted by it. Or so they liked to think then.

Belushi always mocked sentimentality, especially phony, self-aggrandizing show-biz sentimentality. While part of a touring company of *The National Lampoon Show,* Belushi would conclude the entertainment by telling the audience, "We only want your money; we don't care about you at all." In a piece he wrote for *The Washington Post* in 1977, Belushi said, "I won't do prime time until the Pryors and the Wilders start calling the shots," referring to comics Richard Pryor and Gene Wilder.

"You know that, but still you turn to me and scream, 'John Belushi, my God, why don't you *do* something? You're the hope of the future of television! Please help us.' No, get off my back! I've done enough. I've got better things to do, like walk down a country road, stop and smell the roses, then pull them out by their roots."

Michaels told an interviewer once that he liked Belushi on the spot, "because he walked into my office and started to abuse me. He said, 'I can't stand television,' and that was just the kind of abuse I wanted to hear."

Maybe the trick is to give one's fair share of abuse as well as to take it. This is a way to let them know you're around.

During a short, eerily prophetic film made for *Saturday Night Live,* Belushi appeared as himself at the kind of ripe old age he would never live to see. He was wandering through a graveyard in winter, looking at the headstones of fellow *SNL* players who had preceded him in death. One, he said, died of a drug overdose. And how had he managed to survive? Because, he explained, "I'm—a dancer!" Then he did a Greek kind of dance among, if not actually on, the graves. It is a pleasure to remember him this way.

His impudence was heroic, his irreverence immaculate. No one has come forth to replace him.

In his black Blues Brothers suit, Belushi often opened a performance with daft, incongruous cartwheels across the stage. He was wickedly agile, especially for a stocky guy, and from the neck up, too; his eyebrows were acrobatic. So in close-up or in long shots, he could be hilarious—capable of subtlety, but usually scoffing at it. John Belushi came and went in a hurry, but he made such a racket that no one will ever have to wonder if he was really here. He was here, all right. He was here.

L A D Y   P E E L

~~~~~~

f Bette Midler or Carol Burnett or Lily Tomlin had looked into the magic mirror and asked who was the funniest woman of them all, it wouldn't have answered with any of their names. The funniest woman of them all was Beatrice Lillie. For a long time, she was billed as "the funniest woman in the world," and nobody sued for false advertising.

For the last fourteen years of her life, however, Beatrice Lillie reigned in exile. A stroke left her partially paralyzed, and she never appeared in public. On the day after her death, at the age of ninety-four, John Phillip Huck, her longtime friend and guardian, died, too. Rather than declare a new funniest woman of them all, it would be wiser to retire the title.

No one else could wear the crown at quite the jaunty angle she did.

All the funny women, and many funny men, are in her debt.

Though she was born in Toronto, Lillie came to be regarded as the epitome of British wit. Her quixotic, stately, knockabout style was hers alone; she was a dignified woman who did undignified things and made them hilarious. A critic for *The New Yorker* said her humor was based on "great elegance continually beset by tiny humiliations."

It was silly, mad, incongruous, wonderful. She sang "There Are Fairies at the Bottom of Our Garden" and "In a Bar on the Piccolo Marina" and "I Heard My Goldfish Yodelling." It was usually triple entendre or nothing.

Lillie had become a huge star long before television arrived, and TV might seem too prosaic a medium for such a chic, specialized talent. But in the fifties, networks considered part of their role to be cultural uplift, and Lillie was featured on many variety shows and "spectaculars," as specials were called then. Years later she appeared with great success on the Jack Paar program, with Paar proving a perfect foil.

On one show, she told Paar a story about having been at the Savoy Grill while the Germans were buzz-bombing London. Everyone ducked onto the floor, she said—ducking onto the floor to illustrate—and the conversations she recalled hearing were, "That's *my* drink! No, that's *my* drink!"

"All we thought about was our drinks."

In fact, the war took her only son, Robert, killed in 1942. She went on to entertain the troops, tirelessly. Her husband, Sir Robert Peel, had died in 1934, leaving her with a title she tended to use self-mockingly: Lady Peel. Paar and others referred to her as Auntie Bea. Whatever one called her, she was the very definition of unique, a thoroughly and singularly legendary dame to rank with Dietrich and Garland and Garbo.

"Bea Lillie has become more than a legend," wrote Elsa Maxwell in 1944. "She is unquestionably the greatest comedienne on the stage today." Lillie had just made her triumphant return to the States, after a five-year absence, in a Billy Rose revue called *The Seven Lively Arts*, which costarred Benny Goodman and Bert Lahr. The top ticket price was an unheard of $24 and the show's budget a then-astronomical $300,000. But the major fuss was reserved for Bea Lillie.

"The perfect clown," said one critic. "She is glorious," said another. And a third wrote, "Seeing her again, it is easy to understand why the British people withstood Hitler's blitz."

On the Paar show, she rose one night for a comic number supposedly detailing her latest and most passionate hobby: "I pick up bits of paper with my toes." Kicking off her shoes to demonstrate, she did a languid and lanky soft-shoe around the stage. For reasons not entirely explainable, it was completely enchanting.

She wore long white gloves and a demure hat. She was, to quote the title of her memoirs, *Every Other Inch a Lady*. One would not correctly have called her a comic or a clown; she was a comedienne, and the muse seemed born in her, not something she could ever have learned or adopted. Maybe it was in the genes, maybe it was in the brain cells; wherever and whatever it was, nobody will ever be able to bottle it and sell it in stores.

If that were possible, then every generation would be able to have Beatrice Lillies of its own.

To see her in person was inevitably and absurdly memorable. In 1964, she starred on Broadway in *High Spirits*, a musical version of Noel Coward's comedy *Blithe Spirit*, about a man haunted by the frisky ghost of a dead wife. The man was played by Edward Woodward, later the star of the CBS series *The Equalizer*. The frisky ghost was Tammy Grimes.

Lillie played Madame Arcati—"I'm a happy medium, it's true"—the eccentric psychic who summons spirits with her beloved Ouija board, to which one of her songs is an ode. The song wasn't particularly clever, but Lillie made it seem so, and every night, not exactly like clockwork, she would romp through encore after encore, halting the plot to lark and gambol, the crowd cheering her on and on and on.

She swooned, she swayed, she camped and cavorted. She didn't just stop the show. She stopped the earth. For a few minutes, anyway.

Appearing on talk shows to plug the musical, Lillie insisted that audiences were entering the theater singing its title song. And then she'd sing, "High spirits, we've got high spirits"—to the tune of "Hello, Dolly," then the big hit on Broadway.

Her film work was scarce; she was best appreciated in person. Anglophiles and fans of smart comedy cherish her work in *On Approval*, made in 1934. Much, much later, she played a rascally landlady who sold flappers into white slavery in the 1967 movie musical *Thoroughly Modern Millie*. She lent the film its only real mirth.

And in 1956, Lillie was the very last of the dozens of cameo players to be seen in Michael Todd's *Around the World in 80 Days*. Lillie played a hell-bent revivalist who stops Phileas Fogg in his tracks as he races the clock to his London club. "The Devil never sleeps, brethren," she says to her small flock. "Even now, as we stand here, he is hurrying some poor soul to his doom." In rushes David Niven as Fogg.

These film performances give only a glimpse of Lillie's pixilated genius. The appearances with Paar and on other TV shows were merely indicative. Those who are old enough to have seen her in revues on the stage speak of such events as if they had been celestial visitations. They will never forget the time she sang an entire aria in her very respectable coloratura soprano and, with an entirely straight face, hiked up her skirt to reveal a pair of roller skates with which she then sped off into the wings. Her humor verged on slapstick, but it remained that, humor, not just comedy. It was always smart and sophisticated and as mischievous as the inextinguishable gleam in her eye. She sent up things that needed sending up.

Beatrice Lillie ruled the stage in an era of richly amusing people, and she was one of the most amusing of all—not only entertaining, which a trained dog can be, but amusing. She had the "talent to amuse" that her friend Coward wrote about in a song, and perhaps—we will never really know—it was part of her outlook on life until the very, very end. As she sang at the conclusion of her one-woman show in the fifties, "The party's over now." Heigh-ho, if love were all!

UNMITIGATED GALL

~~~~~~
~~~~~~

W ith a Soviet dictator, a network blockhead, a feisty feminist, or a bothersome windmill, David Susskind always went the full fifteen rounds. He rattled bars, he made noise, he let his feelings be known, and there were many. The world is quieter, and duller, without him. David Susskind is most vividly remembered as the host of his own syndicated talk show, a forum in which he vented opinions left and right and elseways. He embarked upon a famous joust with guest Nikita Khrushchev in 1960 that made everybody mad.

But his greater contribution to television was as a producer, a forceful holdover from the live "golden age" of the TV fifties, a man attracted to projects of class and significance, be they a

Glass Menagerie with Katharine Hepburn, a *Death of a Salesman* with Lee J. Cobb and Mildred Dunnock, or the acclaimed urban drama series *East Side, West Side* with George C. Scott and Cicely Tyson.

On a trip to Washington years ago for the taping of a one-man show on Lincoln that he produced, Susskind considered the caliber of television entertainment at that time and, in full huff, declared, "To watch this aimless drivel violates my code of morality."

He had a code of morality.

That's part of what made him old-fashioned.

Old-fashioned, and yet never out of date. He was always plugged in, and full of electricity. At the taping of *Mister Lincoln,* he would dash from the TV trailer outside Ford's Theatre and into the house and back again, barking instructions and doling out encouraging praise and fussing demonstratively over every detail. He was a hands-on producer.

On his talk show, originally called *Open End* and later *The David Susskind Show,* the host blazed trails both critical and trivial. He discovered transsexuals long before Phil Donahue did, for instance, but he also opened his video salon to celebrated thinkers in the arts and politics.

His encounter with Khrushchev was both praised and derided in its time, but most viewers had to concede that Susskind had held his own. A right-wing sponsor angrily pulled its commercials off the program on the grounds that a Communist leader should not be given airtime, and a Washington TV station refused to broadcast the interview live, so other cities saw it before viewers in the nation's capital could.

Years later, some stations relegated Susskind's talk show to very wee hours where few could see it. But those who did can hardly have found it uneventful. Susskind drew considerable heat for his recalcitrance in the face of onrushing feminism, but he liked to point out that Germaine Greer began one of their on-air wrestling matches by asking him, "Would you be interested to know that I have no underpants on?"

The program was intellectual by contemporary talk-show standards, yet not staid. One installment, "How to Be a Jewish Son," brought together Mel Brooks, David Steinberg, and other American wits for a ninety-minute gabfest that became a television comedy classic, far funnier than much scripted humor of its day.

And while he made his mark on television with such illustriously tony productions as *Eleanor and Franklin* and a riveting version of *The Iceman Cometh* with Jason Robards (on Susskind's landmark *Play of the Week* anthology series), Susskind called himself a "pragmatist" who could think commercial as well, and did when he helped bring to TV the winningly absurd spy spoof *Get Smart!* with Don Adams.

"What nobody seems to appreciate about me is that I have an excellent sense of humor," he complained once. "Why don't they ever say, 'God, that guy is funny?' I'm really very funny!" He also described himself then as someone with "a finely honed intelligence from a lot of living, and reading, and some travel," and as "really a very nice person."

What Susskind epitomized was a breed of television producer now almost vanished—the kind who has faith in the medium and its capacity to enlighten, not just preoccupy, an audience. He saw television as a marvelous instrument, not a cash register with a screen. He brought happy passion to his work, and he believed that even a mere television program could illuminate and ennoble.

David Susskind wasn't given much to modesty. And he

needn't have been. He will be remembered for many of his productions, not the least of which was his own life. He had standards, he had commitment, he wanted to help make television better. And since he should certainly be entitled to a last wish, let it also be said: God, that guy was funny.

K U K L A P O L I T A N   L I F E

When Burr Tillstrom died, he took most of an entire repertory company with him. Indeed, he took more than that. For those of a certain age, those who are members of the first American television generation, Tillstrom's death severed a last link with childhood and with television's own bright youth.

It was once a magic box.

Kukla, Fran and Ollie, the program that Tillstrom created and performed, was pure magic and pure television. It was more than another children's show: Tillstrom never liked Kukla, Ollie, Beulah Witch, Madame Oglepuss, and the other Kuklapolitans referred to as mere "puppets." We rarely saw more of Tillstrom than his arms from about the elbows out, swathed in one of his creations, or the quick hello cameo he might do at the end of the show, but through the characters we knew him, and he made himself worth knowing.

Fran Allison, sole visible nonpuppet member of the troupe, who would saunter out to the miniature proscenium for each day's adventures, says she came to regard the Kuklapolitans as real, just as those in the loyal audience did. "Kukla and I of course had a beautiful love affair—I adored him, and he adored me—but I loved all of them," she says, in the rosy, liquid voice she always had.

Kuklapolitans weren't preoccupied with the mission of rendering moral tales through television. This was an easygoing, relaxed, conversational show, the epitome of what was then considered the Chicago school of television.

"We made up television," Tillstrom told author Max Wilk. "There was no influence to teach us. We weren't conforming to anything. California never bothered to develop any television techniques; they just adapted films to television. But Chicago in those days was a very special place."

The Kuklapolitan Players were as gifted a repertory company in their way as any that ever trod a board; they were the Old Vic and the Savoyards, and the chorus of cutups on *The Jack Benny Show*. But *Kukla, Fran and Ollie* was more than theater. It was group therapy, an education in sensitivity for kids and their parents at home, a daily essay in the shrewdest, gentlest sort of observational humor. During particularly tender years, it may have seemed to us we learned as much about life from Kukla, Fran, and Ollie as from any other source.

This was one case of television delivering us into good hands.

Like the new medium, Tillstrom's art was nothing if not spontaneous. He didn't use scripts, in part, he explained, because he couldn't turn the pages when both hands were working puppets. Instead, Fran and the company would talk and sing and cope and make it up as they went along. The program was live in the fullest sense. It was real in the fullest sense. It was maximum minimalism.

The show began on WBKB in Chicago in 1947 but moved the following year to NBC-owned WMAQ, where it thrived. "I remember it was on a Thursday afternoon that the head of the station first talked to Burr about doing a show," Fran Allison recalls. She was a radio star at the time, playing Aunt Fanny, among other characters, on *Don McNeill's Breakfast Club*. On the following Monday morning, Allison says, she and Tillstrom met in a coffee shop to talk about the first day's program and consider the wisdom of the venture. "Burr and I decided it would certainly be worth a try," she says. "We went on the air at four o'clock that afternoon and stayed on for ten years."

During the first year, the Kuklapolitans did an hour of television a day, five days a week, and never once did they show, or even entertain the thought of showing, a cartoon. Musical performances were added along the way, supervised by Jack Fascinato. Once installed at WMAQ, the show went out over what existed at the time of the NBC Television Network, as a daily half hour at 7:00 P.M. RCA, owner of NBC, owner of WMAQ, wanted to move television sets out of the nation's saloons and appliance-store windows and into its living rooms. "They thought a good approach would be through children, because if children like something and want it, and their parents can afford it, they'll probably buy it for them," Fran says.

Kukla was a pragmatic but sentimental Pierrot with a bald head and a large polka-dot nose. Oliver J. Dragon was his pal, a flirtatious reptilicus erectus with long, soulful eyelashes and one wobbly tooth at the end of his snout. Madame Oglepuss, first name Ophelia, was a snooty aspiring diva with a pincushion bosom, and Beulah Witch a sassy battle-ax who flew on a broomstick. Others in the cast included Fletcher Rabbit, Ollie's cousin Dolores, and Cecil Bill, who spoke in a language of his own: "Doo doo doo doo doo doo." And so on.

Nobody talked about "superstars" then, but few stars were so super. The Kuklapolitans practiced, without preaching, gentleness long before there were any consumer watchdog groups to mandate it, and long before Mr. Rogers or *Sesame Street* or the Muppets. Tillstrom wore his heart on his sleeves in a sense, maybe *as* his sleeves, but the program never congratulated itself for being warm and humane. It just was.

Producer Nick Aronson first met Tillstrom in 1973, he says, and became a friend. "He was absolutely remarkable in terms of his talent and his sensitivity," Aronson says. "No one was able to communicate the way he could. Sometimes he might have trouble with one-on-one communication himself, but with the Kuklapolitans he had no trouble at all."

Tillstrom could make the characters real to the audience because they were real to him.

In 1983, the Museum of Broadcasting in New York paid tribute to Tillstrom and his Kuklapolitans, all of whom showed up to conduct seminars and host screenings. Robert Batscha, director of the museum, remembers Tillstrom's visit fondly. "The shows never had any scripts, of course, and he didn't use a script here, either," Batscha says. "He would go behind the booth and pull out his characters, and it was extraordinary how he would adapt to the audience and be funny and clever and witty."

Kukla, Fran, and Ollie became icons of the fifties, like Ike or Elvis or the NBC peacock. They ventured away from their Kuklapolitan Playhouse in Chicago's massive Merchandise Mart, where the WMAQ studios were located, on various special missions. Allison recalls that one of them was to Washington in the very early fifties, to help RCA demonstrate its compatible color television system for members of Congress and other mover-shakers. *Kukla, Fran and Ollie* was one of the first programs in color. "When we got to Washington, I remember Burr showed me he'd had a new Kukla made," Allison recalls. "I was shocked. A new Kukla? Burr said, 'Well Fran, be reasonable. I have to do this for color.' And you know, I was self-conscious with the new Kukla for the first couple of days."

The Kuklapolitans also made guest appearances on other shows, one of them the most momentous of all fifties spectaculars, *The Ford 50th Anniversary Show*, which was broadcast on two networks simultaneously on June 16, 1953.

While appearances by the Kuklapolitans grew sporadic in the sixties, Tillstrom was a semiregular on the American version of *That Was the Week That Was*, on NBC in the 1964–65 season. He introduced his concept of hand ballet, the most memorable example of which was a pantomime of two people meeting during a momentary relaxation of security at the Berlin Wall. Burr Tillstrom was still demonstrating how the seeming limitations of television could be turned into gold.

On the Ford anniversary show, Marian Anderson sang "He's Got the Whole World in His Hands." Oscar Hammerstein II talked with Edward R. Murrow about the perils of the nuclear age. And Ethel Merman sang a now-legendary medley duet with Mary Martin. After Merman finished "There's No Business Like Show Business," Kukla and Ollie appeared.

"There's no business like television, either," Ollie observed.

"It's so *young*, you know," said Kukla.

"Yes," said Ollie peevishly. "When will it grow up?"

VOICE OF AMERICA

America has had many voices, and for a time one of the loudest was Kate Smith's. It was a big, bold, all-embracing voice, and it sang us sentimental songs, and picker-uppers, and at least one invocation: "God Bless America." Kate Smith's long career in records, radio, and television was one marked by so many dramatic comebacks after tragic setbacks that she became a resilient symbol, a national beacon.

Her comebacks took many forms. In the late sixties, she proved herself hip and good-humored by appearing on the Smothers Brothers' show and *Rowan & Martin's Laugh-In.* In the seventies, she became a good-luck charm for the Philadelphia Flyers, who compiled an enviable record of wins when Kate Smith sang "God Bless America" at the Spectrum before their hockey games.

Her trademark tune on the radio was "When the Moon Comes Over the Mountain," which continues, "ev'ry beam brings a dream, dear, of you." But it was Irving Berlin's "God Bless America" that she introduced in 1938 and sang into the national consciousness, performing it in the film *This Is the Army* (with Ronald Reagan and George Murphy) and using it as the finale to such momentous personal appearances as a cheering, sold-out Carnegie Hall concert on November 2, 1963.

The line most quoted in the wake of her death was one spoken by FDR when he introduced her to King George VI and Queen Elizabeth during their visit to the United States. Roosevelt said, "This is Kate Smith; this is America."

She was not only enormously popular; she was, indeed, enormous. She started her career as the target of fat jokes in Broadway comedies, and reportedly wept in her dressing room after some of those performances. Later, on good advice, she dropped the comedy and opened her arms and sang. In a way, her career came full circle, for in the sixties and seventies, her name became a stock reference in fat jokes by comedians.

By then, though, she was able to discuss her weight matter-of-factly with interviewers, and went on diets that would see her lose as much as ninety pounds. Once, after losing so much weight that no one recognized her, she told a reporter how she put the weight back on eating chocolate sundaes so that people would speak to her on the street again. She carried a photograph of her thinner self in her wallet.

Heftiness was no problem for her fans. A voice that huge had to come from somewhere; it was no peep. Despite its size and a tendency toward bombast, that voice was also capable of subtlety and tenderness. Maybe we kids who grew up to the sound of Kate Smith's voice privately felt that this was what Mom would sound like if only Mom could sing. If all the Moms could sing together.

After becoming a star on radio, Kate Smith graduated, if that is the word, to television with *The Kate Smith Hour* in 1950, and returned in 1960 with *The Kate Smith Show.* In between, there were specials, like one on ABC in April of 1957 that featured guest stars Edgar Bergen and Charlie McCarthy, Ed Wynn, Boris Karloff, Gertrude Berg, and Benny Goodman.

Smith told an interviewer in 1966, "I waited and I watched television for five years before I went on. I waited until they had the bugs worked out. I watched what other performers did wrong, and then I profited by their mistakes."

By then, Kate Smith had already compiled a list of hardships and personal ordeals that would have crushed a frail spirit. Her manager and mentor Ted Collins died in the early sixties, and soon after, Smith herself was badly injured in a fall through a glass shower door. In 1976, she suffered brain damage during a diabetic coma, and in 1980 news stories about Smith contained allegations that she had become the all-but-penniless victim of "mooching relatives."

This time, there would be no comeback, except for a brief personal appearance at the White House in 1982 to accept the Medal of Freedom from the president who'd been a costar four decades earlier. She was weak and thin and confined to a wheel-chair. But something of the old pluck remained. She wore a yellow corsage and pearls. President Reagan said, "Kate always sang from her heart, and so we always listened with our hearts."

Onstage, Kate Smith stood regally, hands clasped beneath Wagnerian bosom; in one hand, sometimes, a then-ladylike handkerchief. She was of a performer-generation that endeav-ored to give the audience all, and then still a little more, and she smiled a broad, buoyant, bolstering smile. When she got to the finale, she belted it out with unapologetic gusto. It looked as if the microphone might tumble to the floor from the sheer force of her voice.

Kate Smith never learned to rock and roll; she could rarely if ever be caught singing the blues. Whatever the opposite of the blues is, that's what she sang. She was from a time in which a performer completing a musical-variety show on television would always thank us for the privilege of coming into our homes.

Moons still come over mountains, and the occasional beam brings a memory of her—a smile, a song, and a voice mountain-sized if not moon-sized. It was a voice that picked you up and filled you up.

This was Kate Smith. This was America.

DOWN AT THE END OF
LONELY STREET

~~~~~~~~~~~~~~~~~~~~~~~~~~~~~~~~~~~~~

or a decade supposedly colorless and plastic, the fifties had a rich pop-cultural iconography. If you wanted to boil the era down to two pivotal phenomena, that would be easy: television, and Elvis Presley.

Between them, they changed almost everything. And some of that changing they did together.

Elvis Presley was one of those few fabled stars who redefine stardom. Elvis also helped redefine popular music, and galvanize a generation. Those who remember their lives having been changed by Elvis are much older now, and they want to remember. They watch *thirtysomething* and remember. They buy compact-disc reissues of rock oldies and remember. And they rally around Elvis almost as if he were still alive, the better to remember him to death.

When the tenth anniversary of his death came, in 1987, it

rather suddenly took on the trappings of a new national holiday, observed annually henceforth, and some of the most fanatical followers were lobbying for an Elvis Presley stamp. He attained a strange dual identity, that of deity on the one hand and kitschy cult totem on the other.

Tabloid headlines were relentless: STATUE OF ELVIS FOUND ON MARS. PAINTING OF ELVIS WEEPS REAL TEARS. CAVEMAN LOOKED LIKE ELVIS. Presley's ghost visited Wayne Newton in Las Vegas according to one (Viva Las Vegas!), and many other sightings were reported. Some continue to insist, seriously or facetiously, that he is still alive and fathering children.

Many celebrities have become bigger in death than they were in life. Elvis threatens to become bigger than anybody.

To see the real Elvis, one doesn't go searching through his films, most of which were not only mediocre but encumbered with a hopelessly homogenized, all-but-neutered Robo-star. To see the real legend behind all the assorted attendant legends, one should consult kinescopes of Presley's earliest TV appearances. There was raw energy for you; there was something electrifyingly original.

Difficult as it may be to believe that it's been well over a decade since Presley died, it's a bit harder, and more painful, to realize that three decades have passed since Presley made his national television debut on *Stage Show*, a half-hour variety series starring Tommy and Jimmy Dorsey (those famous rock-sters) and produced as a warm-up for *The Jackie Gleason Show*.

Presley walked onto the Dorsey brothers' stage, and wriggled hip-deep into the American mainstream, on January 28, 1956. He sang "Blue Suede Shoes" and "Heartbreak Hotel." In musical and cultural terms, it was like the splitting of the atom or the invention of the light bulb. Or the premiere of *Saturday Night Live*. All hell broke loose. And all heaven.

Even though most of its members had yet to reach adolescence, it was a supreme instant of affirmation for the baby-boom generation. The teenager was born with Presley's ascendancy as much as with James Dean's demise. Television would subsequently supply a virtually ceaseless procession of role models, heroes, heroines, and Peck's Bad Persons. Elvis was Peck's baddest. He made the young girls cry; he made them scream as they had never screamed before.

The bobby-soxers of the forties who squealed for Sinatra were to be outdone. Elvis of the baby face and the impertinent gyrations—so allegedly lust-inducing that he was photographed only from the waist up during one of his appearances on *The Ed Sullivan Show*—spoke to and exploited something heretofore untapped.

Male sex symbolism was among the things that would never be the same. Certainly men's haircuts wouldn't. Elvis introduced plumage. Until him, it was absolutely unheard of that a man, a mere man, would cause an uproar on television by seeming too sexy. All the attention had been focused on Faye Emerson's cleavage, and on other celebrity bosoms. Elvis deflected the gaze elsewhere. He gave young America something gratifying and intimately scandalous with which to agonize parents.

Elvis and television used each other brilliantly. The provocative collaboration was strikingly recalled in a documentary by Alan and Susan Raymond called *Elvis '56*, a portrait of Presley at his moment of emergence. They brought that moment back so vividly one began to feel as though maybe cars still had fins and Cokes cost a nickel.

Through rare, full-length reprises of Presley TV appearances, backstage and newsreel footage, and a collection of black-and-white photographs by Alfred Wertheimer, the Raymonds invoked Elvis and his time.

When Elvis speaks, sings, and sways for himself, he clarifies the appeal of the performer and the style he was helping to create—and shows how alien this new creature was. There was an attempt in Las Vegas to pair him with Freddy Martin and his creamy ballroom dance tunes. Elvis clowned with another great fifties oddity, Liberace, and brother George. Some of the old clips seem still rivetingly raunchy today, even though we've now lived through such outrageous progeny of Elvis as Prince and Billy Idol. On *The Milton Berle Show*, Elvis sang "Hound Dog," and, just when it seemed the song was over, launched into a couple of lascivious bonus choruses. Good grief, what a display. One has to be at least slightly awestruck.

In still pictures, contrastingly, Elvis looks like the all-American virgin. He's not just a white boy; he's practically alabaster. America is fascinated by the sight of corrupted innocence— hence the lingering fixation on Marilyn Monroe.

The juxtaposition, that's what we love. The living irony. Do we read too much into these old pictures because we know what would come later? We probably knew, or almost knew, what would come later even back at the beginning. It's the old story, but it suffers nothing from retelling. Elvis retold and relived it in garish and yet wrenching terms.

In Elvis now we see a metaphor for Things Gone Wrong, and such public sacrificial displays as his offer a kind of solace from things gone wrong in one's own cosmos. Down at the end of lonely street, it's actually very crowded.

Elvis became terribly controversial after his Berle show appearance, and when it came time for a *Steve Allen Show* gig, Allen felt it necessary to assure the audience (and nervous sponsors), "We want to do a show the whole family can enjoy," and then introduce "the new Elvis Presley," virtually immobilized and dressed in black tie and tails.

He sang "Hound Dog" to a basset hound that wore a top hat, arguably a degrading spectacle, though Elvis appears to have found it funny. He wasn't pretentious and self-worshiping as rock stars are now. Even in the most seemingly carnal-minded of Presley's TV performances, there's a self-effacing smile on his face, an infectious youthful cheer.

After the mid-fifties, Presley's television appearances were rare, but he never could have had the blinding instant impact he had without TV; it put him over as it has put over innumerable stars, fashions, habits, sayings, mouthwashes, and washday miracles since. It is estimated that a total of 1.5 billion people worldwide eventually saw Elvis's 1973 *Aloha From Hawaii* special during its several telecasts.

Television was there at the creation, and of course it was there at the conclusion. The day Elvis died is legendary in TV circles for reasons other than its musical and sociological significance. In a classic and notorious blunder, CBS editors and producers decided not to lead with the story of Presley's death on that night's edition of *The CBS Evening News with Walter Cronkite*, choosing instead a Panama Canal report.

ABC led with Elvis on *ABC Evening News* with Harry Reasoner and Barbara Walters. NBC led with it on *NBC Nightly News* with David Brinkley and John Chancellor, and Brinkley anchored a late-night NBC News special as well.

CBS knew almost immediately that the judgment call had been a stupendous wrong-o. It was seen as a sign that those behind the broadcast were old hat and out of touch, certainly unaware of the effect a pop phenom like Presley could have on uncountable millions of lives, as well as on the course of American culture.

Lane Venardos, then Washington producer for *Evening News*, recalls the gaffe with chagrin: "It caused no small amount of consternation, and in our drive to set things right, we gave considerable attention to the memorial service that was held in Memphis a few days later."

Vernardos himself was sent to Memphis to supervise the coverage, and remembers asking the cab driver at the airport to drive past Graceland on the way into town. "I saw people from every conceivable walk of life, young, old, everything. Some held candles. I saw women with tears streaming down their faces. Then it hit me how much this affected people."

For years afterward, whenever an important figure died, the word at CBS was "Remember Elvis," a warning not to underestimate the story. Indeed, *The CBS Evening News* went overboard when John Lennon was shot and overplayed the story out of Elvis guilt.

Reminders of Elvis were never far from the television lens, whether it was Andy Kaufman's inspired impression on *Saturday Night Live,* the much-discussed army of Elvis impersonators at the 1986 "Liberty Weekend" pageant or, currently, a lavishly sideburned professional wrestler who bills himself as "Honky-Tonk Man." An icon is subjected to myriad permutations. Poor Elvis has gone through many.

In its most banal state, his life is interpreted as another fable about the wages of success and the toll taken by celebrity. Rock music fell under the control of producers and technicians, and the foundations laid by Presley and his fellow pioneers were buried under layers of digital gingerbread and chintzy glitz. Sissy rock came later.

It's hard to contemplate the Presley story without drifting into the soap-opera semantics favored by a persistent surviving contingent of his fans—and, it would appear, their offspring. One of the last clips in *Elvis '56* is from his January 6, 1957, appearance on *The Ed Sullivan Show.* Although he sang a raucous

"Don't Be Cruel," he also sang a movingly unaffected "Peace in the Valley," a spiritual from his youth.

His youth became our youth and his songs our songs. Because he emerged just as television emerged, they both entered the consciousness when it was in a kind of dreamlike state—unguarded, young, susceptible. It's highly doubtful that the planets will ever be lined up in just such a configuration again.

~~~~~~
~~~~~~

Don't look," said a man in the fifteenth row to his wife, and she immediately closed her eyes. Oddly enough, that was a tribute to the director whose film was on the screen. Janet Leigh had just stepped into the shower and turned on the spray, and through the translucent curtain a menacing figure could be seen entering the bathroom. The film was *Psycho* and the director Alfred Hitchcock, at that moment sitting in a box and watching the scene with the twenty-eight hundred other people who'd come to Lincoln Center for a gala in his honor.

In film clip after film clip came image after image of anxiety, peril, and mayhem. Cary Grant and Eva Marie Saint scampered down the noses of Mount Rushmore; Farley Granger slugged it out with Robert Walker on a runaway merry-go-round; Joseph Cotten tried to push Teresa Wright off a speeding train; and

Grace Kelly stabbed Anthony Dawson in the back with a large pair of scissors in an attempt, quite successful, to keep him from strangling her to death.

When all this ended and the house lights came up, the crowd rose to its feet cheering and applauding the director. Finally he stood up, as if about to make a speech, and the audience was silent. And all Hitchcock said to them was, "As you have seen on the screen, the scissors is the best way."

A master self-publicist as well as the master of suspense, Alfred Joseph Hitchcock nevertheless remained terse and elusive whenever asked about the deeper meanings that might have been lurking in his films. He loved discussing technique—how he created the illusion of a flooding cockpit for a plane crash in *Foreign Correspondent*—but not the films' subtexts, nor even whether there were any. Asked years after its release to analyze *The Birds,* in which feathered friends inexplicably turn into flocked fiends, Hitchcock would only say something silly like, "It was very simple. They had rabies."

But in many of his fifty-three movies, especially the darker and more haunting ones, it does seem Alfred Hitchcock was trying to tell us something—mainly, that we don't stand a chance. You could be sitting in a hotel bar with friends having a quiet drink and be mistaken for somebody else, then kidnapped, poured full of bourbon, and sent down a winding mountain road in a stolen Mercedes. And the next thing you know, you're running for your life.

You could be in the wrong place on the wrong night and find you are the wrong man, jailed for someone else's crime. You could be on vacation and discover that the last whispered words of a dying man have put you and your family in mortal danger. You could accidentally bump into a stranger on a train and be helplessly drawn into a madman's double murder plot. You could be sitting there in your own house, minding your own business, and suddenly find that crows and seagulls were massing outside with the intention of crashing through your windows and pecking your eyes out.

And any of this even before you've had your morning coffee. The settings in most of these films were prosaic, the people ordinary, but the circumstances fantastic. The message was clear: Life is itself life-threatening. Hitchcock liked to dangle people: James Stewart dangled from a rooftop in *Vertigo*, and dangled from a ledge with a cast on his leg in *Rear Window*; Cary and Eva dangled together in *North by Northwest*; Norman Lloyd (later a producer of Hitchcock's TV show and, still later, a regular on *St. Elsewhere*) dangled from the Statue of Liberty's torch in *Saboteur*. The imagery of course exploits the fear of falling. But also the fear of dangling.

It was said that the plights of such characters symbolized the disorientation and anxiety unique to the twentieth century, that many of Hitchcock's films were distinctively twentieth-century horror stories. Hitchcock wouldn't cop even to that one. He said he didn't think the twentieth century was more hazardous than the other nineteen. "Why, look at the Victorian Age. Look at poor Jane Eyre, locked up in that house and all manner of things done to her."

His irrepressible facetiousness was put to good use when he hosted, from 1955 to 1962, the anthology series *Alfred Hitchcock Presents* on network television. Each week he began the program by striding out in portly silhouette and taking his place inside a whimsical self-caricature, which he sometimes gave as an autograph. Then he greeted the audience with a polite if portentous "Good evening." A practical joker in his private life and one of the most influential pranksters in the history of cinema, Hitchcock, with his macabre irreverence, might actually have liked the fact that after his death he was symbolically exhumed, subjected to computer colorization, and propped up again on film to host newly produced episodes of the TV series that bears his name.

He went before the cameras in most of his movies, too, becoming briefly that which he frequently disparaged: an actor. Part of the overall joke was a series of puckish cameos; he would be getting off a train with a bass fiddle, or walking a couple of poodles down the street, or racing up to a bus only to have its door close in his face.

To publicize some of his films, he also starred in trailers, or previews, released a few weeks in advance of the picture. For *The Birds*, he delivered a seemingly solemn ornithological lecture. For *Psycho,* he conducted a lengthy tour of the movie's creepy backlot set—the looming gingerbread house on the hill over the squalid Bates Motel. And in the trailer for *Frenzy*, which marked his return to England after decades of making films in the United States, Hitchcock was discovered floating on his back down the Thames River, a moderately animated corpse.

For all the disorder he brought into the lives of characters on the screen, Hitchcock prized orderliness above all else in his daily life. Many of the actors who worked on his films claim to have seen him asleep in the director's chair at the end of a take. He was either faking and trying to be funny, or he really could have lost interest in what was being filmed, since he said the most enjoyable part of filmmaking for him was planning the movie out, shot by meticulous shot. Only commercials are shot this meticulously anymore.

Hitchcock's office on the Universal lot was an incongruous little Cape Cod bungalow. Inside, all was calm and neat, and Alfred Hitchcock would sit at his ornate vast desk looking like a strawberry dressed for a funeral. His pink face and pink hands were the only signs of color. To a visitor in 1977, he obligingly demonstrated a pacemaker that had been inserted in his chest a couple of years before. He unbuttoned his shirt and showed off the small round raised area of skin that covered the pacemaker, and he showed how he could check on his heartbeat by holding some sort of magnet up to it and dialing a special phone number, then waiting for a series of buzzes and beeps. The device amused him—an implanted symbol of his mortality.

Being in that office with Hitchcock was like walking into a painting by Magritte. Something was intriguingly, mischievously askew. Hitchcock, no matter how entertaining and commercial his movies, was an artist, and his work bears a stamp every bit as distinctive as that of Poe, Orwell, Kafka, or Wilde, at times resembling all of them. He wasn't just scaring people, or even just thrilling them. He was leading them into a realm they could normally reach only through dreams.

No other director has been so imitated, or paid so much cinematic homage. François Truffaut, a Hitchcock worshiper, made *The Bride Wore Black* as a tribute. Brian De Palma's *Obsession*, *Sisters*, and *Body Double* mimic *Vertigo*, *Psycho*, and *Vertigo* again. Jonathan Demme made *The Last Embrace* à la Hitch. And Mel Brooks paid a satirical tribute with *High Anxiety*. Asked how he reacted when films by others were labeled "Hitchcockian," Hitchcock said, "I do prefer them to say 'Not as good as.' Or, 'Hardly up to the standard of.'"

Hitchcock was joking. But none were as good as, or up to the standard of. Alfred Hitchcock was one of the few filmmakers to become his own genre.

On the day of the Lincoln Center gala in 1974, as he sat in a hotel suite overlooking Central Park, Hitchcock—who'd bumped off dozens of characters in his films over the years—was asked about his views of the hereafter, of heaven and hell. "I can't believe in them in the material sense—fire and brimstone and all that," he said. "But I do believe that something of us survives after death. The mind survives. The voice certainly survives, in sound waves that may never stop once they enter the world. How long do they go on? Forever. It's like tossing a pebble into the water. The ripples go on and on and on. You say they stop at the shore, and I say, there is no shore. The voice of Henry VIII could still be floating around in the air for all we know."

He sat composed and motionless as he spoke, except for making a small circular gesture with his hand when he talked about the ripples in the water.

Another interviewer once asked Hitchcock to describe his idea of happiness. He replied, "A clear horizon. No clouds, no shadows, nothing."

FLEETING WISP
OF GLORY

ome say his Hamlet was among the best of the century.
But the role most will remember him playing is the role
of Richard Burton. He played it to the virtual and literal
hilt, gallivanting across the gossip pages of the civilized
world with a style that is now, sadly, out of style.

We saw Richard Burton as self-destructive but in a
romantic, worldly, seen-it-all, done-it-all way. His biographer,
Melvyn Bragg, said Burton was afflicted with "an unbearable
melancholy" most of the time, but called his "an epic life." It
often seemed, indeed, an open book.

He was an engaging figure, self-mocking and sophisticated,
reminiscent of kindred-spirit drinkers like John Barrymore and
such literary imbibers as fellow Welshman Dylan Thomas.
There was poetry in the soul and roguishness in the eyes, anyone
could see that. And hear it. That voice, that voice; it came up

from just below Middle Earth, sepulchral and reverberant. Burton's voice was so glorious that on the soundtrack of the TV documentary series *Winston Churchill: The Valiant Years*, Burton proved he was probably the only human being who could make Churchill's words sound even better than Churchill did.

Burton had valiant years of his own. Or perhaps only valiant days and nights, but those count, too.

He could speak the grand words and make them grander, and double the loftiness of lofty thoughts: a Man for All Seasons. And yet, by contrast, there was always this other life he lived in the columns, usually in connection with his occasional wife and, we all believed, One True Love, Elizabeth Taylor. Tales of their tiffs, tipplings, topplings, and tussles were instant gourmet folklore, and their chaotic romance a continuing juicy serial. This was royal gossip, on a plane so much higher than chatter about television stars or pop singers.

It helped that even while professing a desire for privacy, the fabulous couple was really quite generous in living the fantasy in public. They did it with tease casting in films like *The Sandpiper*, *Anthony and Cleopatra*, *The V.I.P.s*, and *The Taming of the Shrew*, films in which the audience was encouraged to imagine it was glimpsing something of the couple's private lives in their movie performances. It's perfect that their last stage appearance together was in *Private Lives*.

Watching *The Sandpiper* now is less like watching an old movie than like reading old fan magazines; it was such a piquant strain of kitsch at the time that it retains a certain fascination. Burton always seemed knowingly bemused and perhaps even delighted by the way the public lapped it up. And so though it was widely said he had never realized his full potential as an actor, or that he squandered his great gift, the word "tragic" would never suit him.

A lot of us are still dazzled by exhibitions of conspicuous excess, and that's the image Burton had off the screen. That's what he seemed to be living out, at least during his salad days—tossed salad days—of the sixties. He didn't seem contemptuous of the fact that more people knew him as playboy than as *the* melancholy Dane, or seriously to begrudge the public its peephole view of his adventures as a lover.

To an even greater extent than his brilliant colleague James Mason, who preceded him in death by mere days, Burton took on movie roles that were leagues beneath him and his acting abilities. In later days, some Burton films were so minor they were barely released, or shelved outright. When he first went to Hollywood, he got roles like that of a pious convert in *The Robe*, the first movie in CinemaScope and one Burton himself later referred to as rubbish. Later, he came full circle to rock bottom in *The Exorcist II*, a ludicrous debacle that had Burton cast again as a priest and tended to send audiences into giggles rather than chills.

And yet there remained the broodingly sonorous and cultivated voice, and an acerbic vitality no matter how shallow the surface. It can be said of Richard Burton that he lent a certain stature to Doing It for the Money.

His best movie performances may have been as a hardened, stricken cynic in *The Night of the Iguana* and as the battered husband, George, opposite Elizabeth Taylor's emasculating Martha in *Who's Afraid of Virginia Woolf?* And though his Hamlet brought him wide acclaim, more theatergoers saw him as King Arthur in *Camelot*, the Lerner and Loewe musical whose title song has now become a signature for the Kennedy years, years we look upon as having been halcyon and graceful and full of hope.

Other actors have played the role since, but none had Burton's singularly majestic way with the words. His is the voice we hear in our minds singing the benediction that ended the musical and seems now to have closed an era: "Ask every person if he's heard the story, and tell him strong and clear if he has not; that once there was a fleeting wisp of glory, called Camelot."

A fleeting wisp of glory, for one brief shining moment. It's as much as anyone can expect. One assumes Richard Burton, true to his Welsh soul, did not go gentle into that good night. One assumes it because he never went gentle into that good day.

~~~~~~

ohn Houseman reigned for years as America's favorite old
grouch. He made old grouches respectable again. He
made it a pleasure to feel a little bit intimidated.

Houseman was not the standard-issue Hollywood old-
timer, not by any means. He wasn't the cute sort of coot
that Shirley Temple might have tickled into merriment,
or the kind of crusty codger played by Walter Brennan. John
Houseman restored dignity to the idea of being old. He was old
and proud of it, and even a youth-obsessed society sensed and
savored that pride.

When he spoke, you believed him. He had roughly the author-
ity of God. And probably the same eyebrows.

That he undertook the new career of acting at the age of
seventy helped make Houseman a commanding and encouraging symbol of longevity and vitality. It didn't hurt, either, that

he won an Oscar for his first major role, that of Professor Kingsfield in *The Paper Chase.*

Though his health finally failed him, it appears his wit never did. A writer, producer, and director before he was an actor, he was clearly no overnight sensation. It might be said of Houseman, in fact it almost has to be said, that fame came to him the old-fashioned way. He earned it.

In person, Houseman was neither an old grouch nor even particularly crabby. He was a warmly accommodating raconteur with the collected anecdotes of a lifetime within reach. Perhaps a relatively easy, unassuming temperament helped him deal with extremely temperamental people. As a producer, he tamed directors; as a director, he tamed producers. As the head of the Juilliard Acting School, he disarmed teachers and pupils alike.

Probably his most legendary volatile collaborator was Orson Welles, with whom Houseman produced the famous hoaxy *War of the Worlds* radio broadcast, a *trompe l'oreille* that scared a nation silly. Houseman died in 1988 a day after the fiftieth anniversary of this landmark in jumping-out-and-saying-boo. After *War* Houseman worked as script editor on the Welles movie classic *Citizen Kane,* which Houseman later suggested might as well have been called *Citizen Welles.*

The scene in which Charles Foster Kane demolishes his wife's bedroom after she's walked out on him was inspired, Houseman said, by a temper tantrum Welles himself threw one night at Chasen's Restaurant in Beverly Hills. He got so mad at Houseman he tossed flaming Sterno cans at him, almost setting the joint on fire.

"Undoubtedly, there was an enormous area of genius there," he said later of the boy wonder, who, unlike Houseman, never grew up. They parted company and did not remain friends, yet never quite became enemies either.

Houseman worked with other fabled directors, including Fritz Lang. "We had awful screaming matches, but it was all in a day's work," Houseman recalled in an interview. "One day I heard Lang yelling, 'You are supposed to be a professional! You are paid to be an actor! You are lazy, you are stupid, you are no good! I don't know why we ever started this picture with you!'

"As I came down the stairs, I saw he was addressing a nine-year-old."

Vincente Minnelli made several pictures with Houseman, including one of Hollywood's best looks at itself, *The Bad and the Beautiful*, about a ruthless, corrupting movie producer. They also traveled around Europe shooting *Lust for Life*, the biography of Vincent van Gogh, at locations where Van Gogh really lived and painted. Minnelli wrote of Houseman, "Few producers could claim to be both tasteful and avant-garde as John could. I found him to be honest and sensitive, and more creative than any producer had any right being."

Houseman was a master catalyst. He was often around when great things were happening. No one could doubt his role in them.

His first movie acting job was a small part in the paranoid thriller *Seven Days in May*; he played a rascally admiral who was part of a military plot to take over the government of the United States. But it was Kingsfield that made Houseman a star, and vice versa. Kingsfield was the teacher every student ever feared and admired, and Houseman took naturally to the role.

The character suffered some diminution when turned into a continuing feature on the TV series version of the film, which started on CBS, went to PBS and then to cable. When on CBS, it and Houseman were favorites of another estimable senior citizen, CBS founder and chairman William S. Paley.

"I'll be 'the professor' into eternity," Houseman once grumbled. But his new professorial image landed him a number of high-paying commercial gigs, the most famous being ads for the Smith-Barney brokerage firm—the ones that always ended with Houseman growling, "They make money the old-fashioned way; they *earn* it."

Houseman's distinctive line-reading became much imitated. It worked its way into the culture, and him with it. In 1982, *Advertising Age* named Houseman "Star Presenter of the Year." His other clients included Puritan cooking oil and Chrysler cars. The irony of his newfound celebrity was not lost on Houseman; he'd been largely invisible to the general audience through decades of significant and innovative work in theater and film, and now he was hugely famous for the way he pitched products on TV.

Most of the characters Houseman played in films qualified as "distinguished," though one of his last appearances was as an embittered, enfeebled intellectual in Woody Allen's soporific *Another Woman*. By the time the film was shot, Houseman's encroaching illness had taken a noticeable toll. He looked ill, yet he was able to summon the passions of a pro.

Houseman knew almost everybody and everything in theater and film, and so was induced to write a memoir, *Runthrough*, that begat two sequels. The books were remarkable for their readable grace and the unobtrusiveness of Houseman's ego.

When television went through its golden age in the fifties, Houseman became active in that, too, producing a few *Playhouse 90* dramas and contributing to a series called *The Seven Lively Arts*. Yes, network television once found time for a series called *The Seven Lively Arts*. It was thought at one time that television would become the eighth.

In 1971, agreeing to be interviewed on the subject of Welles and their long-expired relationship, Houseman was free of rancor and regret. He in fact defended Welles against the common charge that the onetime renaissance man had squandered his gifts through lack of discipline.

"I still get infuriated when people say of him, 'Now, what happened?'" Houseman said. "What happened was, he lived his life. It would have been nice if, like Verdi, he had come up with a masterpiece in his old age and, I don't know, maybe he will. But I think he's lived pretty much the way he wanted to live."

The same assessment fits Houseman: He lived his life—a prodigiously full one—pretty much the way he wanted to live it. Did he come up with a masterpiece in his old age? You might say he became one.

~~~~~~

omeday, perhaps tomorrow, we will have to explain to young generations what a "movie musical" was. We won't be able to do that without invoking the name of Vincente Minnelli. He was, said his colleague and friend Alan Jay Lerner, "the greatest director of motion picture musicals the screen has ever known."

So closely and inextricably is Minnelli identified with MGM musicals that when reporting his death, a New York TV station credited him with directing the ebullient satire *Singin' in the Rain*. That was one of the few illustrious MGM musicals Minnelli did not direct. He did, however, direct *Gigi, The Band Wagon, Brigadoon*, and, in 1944, *Meet Me in St. Louis*, the musical that even people who don't love musicals love.

St. Louis starred Judy Garland, later Mrs. Minnelli (one of four wives) and mother of Liza Minnelli. Although the director was a show-biz sophisticate who had arrived in Hollywood from a successful art director's career in New York, he was able to make *St. Louis* a lovingly homey homage to American small-town life, remarkable for its warmth and clarity.

A lot of movies were celebrating fundamental Americana during World War II, but it is Minnelli's elegantly idealized vision that seems to hold up best after the passage of four varyingly tumultuous decades. The film's depiction of turn-of-the-century St. Louis now evokes both the fearfulness and the hopefulness of America during the war.

Minnelli directed straight dramatic films, too, but the trademark fluidity of his camera made even his nonmusicals somehow musical. The high point of *Madame Bovary* was a deranged waltz in a mirrored ballroom that ended with all its windows being smashed. *The Bad and the Beautiful* included an audacious interlude in which Lana Turner threw a hysterical fit while driving down a rainy road, and although she's certainly not singing, the scene could be considered one of the greatest melodramatic arias ever staged for a film.

It is an aria for actress and camera, and Vincente Minnelli was the conductor.

In his autobiography, *I Remember It Well*, Minnelli recalled his technique for getting the optimal performance out of Turner, who he felt was among those who underrated her abilities as an actress. After each long take of the very difficult scene, Minnelli would assure Turner that her work had been just right but that the camera or the lighting or the sound equipment had malfunctioned, and would she please do it again.

Minnelli was never known as a bully or a tyrant. In person he seemed quiet, elfin, soft-spoken and self-effacing, and he talked largely in fragments of sentences. One could tell he must have used more psychology than tyranny to rule a movie set. "Always you had to deal with temperaments," he recalled. "You had to find ways of dealing with each one. I never had any trouble finding a way. All actors are insecure."

Perhaps his finest dramatic film was *Lust for Life*, the story of another brilliant Vincente—van Gogh—with Kirk Douglas playing the tortured artist. Even if his marriage to Judy Garland was among the legendary fiery matchups of Hollywood, Minnelli probably could not be considered "tortured," and yet *Lust for Life* is very much one artist's tribute to another.

Lowering the boom of "art" on Minnelli's films during his lifetime might have sounded pretentious. It would also have threatened to take some of the vitality out of them. But in time, perhaps tomorrow, he'll be afforded the kind of respect that college professors lavish on nineteenth-century novelists now.

There was a lot of art-imitating-life in Minnelli's career. Betty Comden and Adolph Green were, in part, lampooning themselves when they wrote the script for *The Band Wagon*, Minnelli's hilarious send-up of solipsists and narcissists in the theater, and the film includes an explosive production number ("Dance, fools, Dance!") that appears to spoof an earlier, similarly bombastic one in Minnelli's *The Pirate*.

When it was determined that actor Leon Ames, who played Papa, should sing with a voice like producer Arthur Freed's in *Meet Me in St. Louis*, Freed himself was recruited for the job; that's his voice on "Through the Years," sung around the parlor piano in the Smith family's living room.

And in his autobiography, Minnelli recalled an incident from his years as little Liza's proud papa that is highly reminiscent of arguably the most charming sequence in *St. Louis*—the spookily treacherous Halloween night of young Tootie, played by Margaret O'Brien.

Liza was costumed as a witch one Halloween in Beverly Hills,

Minnelli wrote; he'd commissioned her costume at the studio. "This was during her serious period, when she wouldn't be laughed at," he recalled, and the child was mortified when at each house her appearance elicited friendly chuckles. "Finally we stopped at Gene Kelly's. His was an award-winning performance. 'A witch! A terrible witch! Save me!' Liza walked home with her pointed witch's chin held high."

To get Margaret O'Brien to cry during the famous snowman sequence of the film—after Garland sings "Have Yourself a Merry Little Christmas"—director Minnelli, he later admitted, had to tell the young actress that her dog had died. Somehow this worked in take after take.

The magic of the movies.

Occasionally, as in the blowhardy *Yolanda and the Thief,* Minnelli's work seemed overwhelmed by decor, not just integrated with it. And while he was spectacularly productive during the forties and fifties, his sixties films were generally lackluster. His last film, *A Matter of Time,* with daughter Liza, came across like some lesser director's imitation of him.

But at the height of his powers he took the big-studio, made-in-Hollywood movie as far as the eye could see, and then a few steps farther. His visions were splashy but not gaudy, his sensibilities romantic but not campy. This was when movies were bigger than life and better than life, and when, if you were in a snit or a funk, you could go into a movie house expecting what you saw on the screen would cheer you, bolster you, and embolden you when it came to facing the fiends and the furies waiting outside.

Even in Minnelli's first MGM feature, *Cabin in the Sky,* there was an astonishment of bold strokes. Minnelli looked back on his first directorial effort in his book: "The studio put on an extra man to teach me the simple techniques of the camera, primarily when to look left or right," he wrote. "Once that simple lesson was learned, I could dispense with the consultant's advice.

"My instincts saw me through."

The progressive dismantling of Metro-Goldwyn-Mayer is all but complete now. What was once Hollywood's grandest studio has become a paper pawn in the dealings of financiers. The works of Minnelli and other great directors are now items in an inventory. But you open the film can, and what you get is still wonder.

In *Cabin in the Sky*, Ethel Waters sings "Happiness Is Just a Thing Called Joe" to a bedridden Eddie (Rochester) Anderson, while a tall, handsome angel stands at the foot of the bed, listening. Waters sings, "Sometimes the cabin's gloomy, and the table's bare, but then he'll kiss me and it's Christmas everywhere," and Minnelli cuts to a shot of the angel slowly disappearing.

There's something lushly cinematic about even this simple little shot. Clearly someone with a keen eye directed it—a keen eye and a soft heart. Vincente Minnelli's instincts saw him through, and up on the screen it was Christmas everywhere.

MAGNIFICENT YANKEE

~~~~~~
~~~~~~

He danced like a virile marionette, held up by invisible silver strings, leading with taut jaw in a brash show of nerve, propelled across the screen by an ever-boyish bravado, bright-eyed and wiry and full of the devil. Top of the world, Ma! Top of the world!

In his sixty-four movies, James Cagney became sixty-four characters, all of whom had some measure of grit and pluck. But in one of those movies, he was not just a character, he was the national character. Many of his films had iconographic moments—the famous if ungracious mooshing of a grapefruit into Mae Clarke's face in *The Public Enemy*, the explosive apocalypse of *White Heat*—but one film is an entire iconography.

It was his favorite film, he said, the one for which he received the Academy Award as Best Actor in 1942. It was *Yankee Doodle Dandy*.

James Cagney died in 1986 in Stanfordville, New York, but in the great mind's eye of the movies, he fights on, he rattles on—in his compelling, news-ticker staccato—and he dances on. He liked to characterize himself as "a journeyman actor," and a simple hoofer who did his job and went home, but along the way, he became a lot more than that. He became, among other things, us, or at least that part of us we liked to point to with pride.

Yankee Doodle Dandy was ostensibly the screen biography of George M. Cohan, but Cagney's audacious magnetism overshadows the role now. And besides, there are so many parallels.

In the film's opening scene, Cagney as Cohan, recalling his youth for "Captain Jack Young" as FDR, says, "I was a pretty cocky kid in those days, a pretty cocky kid." Through tough-guy role after tough-guy role, Cagney had personified the pretty cocky kid on the screen, and he would later recall that for one of seven children growing up on the streets of New York, cockiness came in handy. The very Cagneyesque move of hunching up his shoulders in a gesture meant to convey macho menace was picked up by Cagney, he said, from an uptown pimp who plied trade at the corner of Seventy-eighth Street and First Avenue in James Cagney's hometown.

Explaining the importance of such trademark body grammar in an interview, Cagney said, "The idea is, if it'll give them something to remember, use it." He grew extraordinarily proficient at giving them something to remember.

FDR awards Cohan the Medal of Honor in *Yankee Doodle Dandy*. Forty-two years after the film was released, James Cagney went to the White House to receive the Medal of Freedom from President Ronald Reagan.

"I'm just a song-and-dance man, everybody knows that," Cohan says to FDR in the movie, and the president replies, "A man may give his life to his country in many different ways, Mr. Cohan, and quite often, he isn't the best judge of how much he has given." Reagan, less noticed at Warner Bros. during the years Cagney ruled its roost, said of Cagney when he gave him the presidential medal, "As a great star at the same studio where I started, he was never too busy to hold out a hand to a young fellow just trying to get under way."

In the closing months of the Reagan administration, Ron and Nancy hosted a screening of *Yankee Doodle Dandy* for forty or fifty invited guests. A. C. Lyles, a producer who knew Cagney well, held up the dancing shoes Cagney had worn in the film and later given him. Reagan recalled that while Cagney was making *Dandy*, there was talk of Reagan's best film, *King's Row*, being pushed by Warners for Oscars that year.

"That was before they got a look at *Yankee Doodle Dandy*," Reagan said. And no, he never begrudged Cagney the Oscar. After he told that story, Reagan sat down and watched the movie again, all the way to the end where Cagney as Cohan dances exuberantly down a White House staircase on the Warner lot.

Cagney could be a sweetheart as well as a roughneck in the movies. He waltzed Rita Hayworth through *The Strawberry Blonde*, one of his lightest and most atypical films. He romped playfully with Ruby Keeler through the campy "Shanghai Lil" number from Busby Berkeley's *Footlight Parade*. He had touching moments as tormented actor Lon Chaney in the film biography *Man of a Thousand Faces*.

But the roles for which Cagney is most celebrated had pronounced abrasive streaks, and there is something in the brashness and heavy mettle that is distinctly American. This was one way we wanted to see ourselves: spunky and confident and unpretentious, ready for anything. That dance down the White House staircase said, "I'm as good as any other guy." There are a lot of things more American than apple pie. But there are not a lot of things more American than James Cagney in *Yankee Doodle Dandy*.

Cagney occasionally played the tough guy who was also a rotter, even after *Dandy* altered his image. His Cody Jarrett in *White Heat* is a homicidal psychotic with a severe Oedipal problem. With customary ingenuousness, Cagney said in later years that the film as written was an ordinary gangster picture until he suggested of the Jarrett character, "Why don't we make him nuts?"

Second in memorability to the "top-of-the-world" finale is a scene in which the jailed Jarrett hears from other convicts whispering down the line at a long mess-hall table that his mother has died. He proceeds to throw a wild, anguished fit that is still frightening to watch, and is dragged from the hall screaming and kicking.

In *Love Me or Leave Me,* he was beastly to Doris Day, as singer Ruth Etting, and in *Mr. Roberts* he was a rancorous, paranoid navy captain, a berserk cartoon cousin to old Warner pal Humphrey Bogart's disturbed Captain Queeg in *The Caine Mutiny*. In Billy Wilder's *One Two Three,* Cagney went all the Cagney mimics one better ("you dirty rat") with a wild, breakneck caricature of himself. At one point, he matches Cagneyisms with impressionist Frank Gorshin.

His whole career seems in retrospect to have been a magnificent dare.

Never a sex symbol, probably no heartthrob, by his own harsh assessment "nothing to photograph," Cagney dominated the screen thanks to the proverbial fire in the belly. You couldn't take your eyes off him. He was like a ticking bomb; he might go off at any minute.

In *Yankee Doodle Dandy,* Cohan is coaxed out of retirement

when young visitors to his farm fail to recognize him, have never even heard of him. Perhaps something like that was responsible for Cagney's reemergence, after two decades of his own retirement, to play the role of the police commissioner in Milos Forman's film of *Ragtime* in 1981. Cagney turned out to be easily the most electric thing in it.

Cagney had come out of hiding earlier, in 1974, to accept the first of the American Film Institute's Life Achievement Awards to be awarded to an actor. In such appearances, he always looked somewhat amazed at the outpouring of affection he received.

Early in 1982, when producer Alexander H. Cohen staged his *Night of 100 Stars* charity gala at Radio City Music Hall, Cagney, though not in the best of health, was persuaded to make another public appearance. It came at the end of a long medley saluting Hollywood. Cagney, who'd been forced to wait in the Music Hall basement through arduous delays in the program, was suddenly whooshed up through a hole in the floor and materialized magically, seated in a chair.

The crowd rose from its seats in a roaring ovation, and Cagney, realizing the cheers were for him, appeared overcome. He bubbled over in tears. This was the high point of the evening. James Cagney was a night of 100 stars all by himself.

"I'm going back to the farm and sit it out," he said to an interviewer shortly before returning to the womb of retirement, though it was interrupted again, briefly, for a CBS movie called *Terrible Joe Moran*, about an aging fighter—which by this time he was. He said he wanted his remaining years to be a time of "no strain" for him. The man who had played so many swaggering upstarts on the screen craved peace and tranquillity.

At least he must have gone back to the farm fully apprised of the high regard in which peers and countrymen held him. "Regard" doesn't quite say it, actually. Hell, we loved the guy. We loved it when he tapped down the marble steps, loved it when he waltzed with the strawberry blonde, loved it when he stood up to demons and when demons got inside him and had to be stood up to by others, loved it when as George M. Cohan he danced up the side of the proscenium in irrepressible exultation.

Something to remember? Who could forget? Yankee doodle, do or die.

～～～～～～～～～～～～～～～～
～～～～～～～～～～～～～～～～
～～～～～～～～～～～～～～～～

he had played the young would-be-princess Anastasia in the movies, but she was more the dowager empress now. The eyes, however, were just the same—plaintive, glistening, accusing. And blue. What a pair of peepers! At sixty-five, Ingrid Bergman was still a radiant beauty, and still a temperamental star.

On this particular afternoon in Beverly Hills, she proved she could still put her foot down with oomph. She decided she had signed enough copies of *My Story,* the autobiography she called "embarrassingly long," and told a publicist, "Well, I'll sign what I can. No, I'm not going to go sit in bookstores! I refuse to go to any more cities."

Then she reclined, more or less, on the couch, and though she'd had two mastectomies, began puffing strenuously on, of all things, Marlboros. Still tough, still tender; still assertive, still submissive. The old one-two. You can see it in her vintage movies on TV. She saw something else. "I run right at the television and stare at it. I think it's fun to see those old movies. And it brings back a lot of happy souvenirs. Many of the people that you see on the screen are gone. I saw *For Whom the Bell Tolls* not too long ago. It was very emotional, because there's hardly anybody left."

And she had awakened early that morning to watch herself on a taped talk show. "What I said was all right, but I don't like the way I look. I always say, 'Where is that youth? What happened to youth?'" She smiled. "It went away, ha-ha."

Actors and actresses are usually intense, but with Ingrid Bergman there was a palpable sense of more so—higher highs, lower lows, smilier smiles, tearier tears. She was asked about the idea that she had been too dependent on men. "Not when it comes to my work," she said. "There, I'm terribly sure. It's very funny; in real life, I'm unsure. I don't know—'Should I do this or should I not?' I follow my heart too much. I lose my head."

On movie sets, she was never hesitant to argue with directors. She argued with Hitchcock: "What he really enjoyed was the preparation of a movie, when he had all those little things on the dining room table—the camera, walls, furniture, and actors. Actors were just little things and they didn't talk back to him. When he placed them there, they stood there. Then, when I came on the set, I started to argue with him. Aw! That wasn't so good. Then his joy was over."

And she argued with Ingmar Bergman on the set of her last theatrical feature, *Autumn Sonata,* for which she got another Oscar nomination. "The way I argue—embarrassing. But of course I thought Charlotte, my character, a very cruel mother, so we had big arguments about that because I cannot possibly imagine a mother staying away for seven years from her child and another child that is paralyzed, plus a grandchild that's given to her—she won't even go to see the grandchild! The grandchild dies, and still she is playing the piano!

"I said, 'Ingmar! This is impossible! And so we argued and argued and finally he said, 'Well, you know, we're not doing *your* life, we're doing Charlotte.' I said, 'Well you must have met many monsters in your life.'"

And, of course, Ingrid Bergman met many monsters in hers. On the screen, she suffered, how she suffered. Charles Boyer tried to drive her insane in *Gaslight*. Claude Rains gave her poison every day in *Notorious* (but Cary Grant carried her down the staircase to safety). Being burned at the stake as Joan of Arc was all in a day's work.

Offscreen, there was also suffering to be done. Strange as it may now seem, the world was shocked in 1948 when Bergman had an affair with Italian director Roberto Rossellini, then married to someone else, abandoning her own husband and child in the process. That she had earlier warmed America's heart playing a nun in *The Bells of St. Mary's* opposite Bing Crosby made her escapade seem to many like a betrayal. Reality was betraying fantasy, and this got her denounced on the floor of the U.S. Senate.

Bergman seemed still to have a lingering bitterness about that, even all those years later. But she said she had none. "At the time, I was terribly hurt. Of course I didn't just shake it off like a duck! I felt guilty. I was sad. I didn't want to work; I just wanted to disappear. Today I look at my beautiful handsome son and I'm very pleased." In time, as Chaplin was forgiven for his little scandals, Bergman was forgiven hers. She returned to Hollywood in 1959 for an Oscar show and was drowned in ovation.

In the sixties and seventies, her roles tended to be on the matronly side. She played a countess in the omnibus movie *The Yellow Rolls-Royce* and a cranky maid in *Murder on the Orient Express*, for which she won a third Oscar. Her last major performance was in the television miniseries *Golda*. The Swedish-born Bergman playing the great Israeli leader Golda Meir? Of course. They had many things in common, or at least one: a surpassing stubbornness. It was a perfect note to go out on.

Bergman said once she was shy as a child, but "I had a lion roaring inside me that wouldn't sit down and shut up." Many years later, she said, "My strength I got from my parents, I think," both of whom died when she was young. "It must be in me. I was given very good health, strong and healthy, and I had a sense of humor. That helps a lot, if you can laugh at yourself when all those problems come. And I have an awful lot of friends. Really, people say, 'Well, how many friends do you have in your life? You can count them on one hand.' Well, I can count with both hands. I have very good friends which I can talk to. That's why I don't have to go to psychoanalysts. I bother my friends instead."

She laughed. At herself.

Of all the roles in all the movies, people will probably best and longest remember Ingrid Bergman for walking into Humphrey Bogart's gin joint in *Casablanca*, the movie where none of the actors quite knew what the ending would be until they shot it. Now, everyone remembers almost everything about it; it stands for all the memories over which people become nostalgic, and for lost loves and moral victories and second chances. The fundamental things apply, as time goes by.

And we remember it for Bergman as Ilsa, caught between head and heart again, vulnerable and imploring and yet steadfast and determined. And those eyes—mirrors of a fascinating soul.

Play it, Sam.

"Oh, I can't remember it, Miss Ilsa. I'm a little rusty on it."

"I'll hum it for you. De dy de dy de dum, de dy de dy de dum. . . ."

We'll always have Paris.

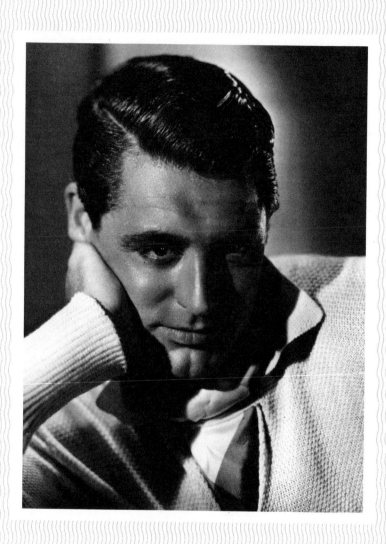

AFFAIR TO REMEMBER

efore there were class acts there was real class. You
know—like Cary Grant. If that was an act, it was a tour
de force. And if Cary Grant didn't always perfectly suit
the roles he played in his seventy-two films, he always
perfectly suited the role of Cary Grant, which is what we
came to see.

Archibald Leach, his real name, continued in this part even
after Cary Grant made his last film, *Walk! Don't Run,* in 1966.
Appearing at charity affairs or glittery social events or White
House state dinners, he always had the gait, the glint, the Cary-
Grantic gleam. One of the ingratiating things about him was
that he appeared genuinely amused at his own stardom and at
the salubrious effect his presence had on other people.

He would tell the author of a gushy, appreciative piece
about him, "You were too kind," and perhaps he really meant

that. Perhaps he thought it was possible to be too kind to Cary Grant.

Words like debonair and elegant come to mind when one thinks of Cary Grant and the handsome figure he cut upon the silver screen in its golden age, but an important part of his enduring career was that he came across as the egalitarian gentleman, an anointed regular guy who went industriously about his assigned task as pop royalty. He was born in England, yes, but the Cockney in his accent linked him to us commoners sitting out there in the dark.

Men could say to themselves, "Yes, if I were Cary Grant, I would behave just that way." And women could say something along the lines of, "Cary, baby, come to Mama." As Pauline Kael has observed, in Cary Grant's films he often played seducee rather than seducer. Grace Kelly chased him all through *To Catch a Thief* (the title had two meanings) and Eva Marie Saint threw herself at him, or as far as she could throw herself in a train compartment, in *North by Northwest.*

Alfred Hitchcock, who made those two films, wanted Grant to play a wife murderer in *Suspicion*; he was just being perverse. Studio bosses ruled that Grant must not be permitted to bump off Joan Fontaine, even if everything in the movie had been pointing toward that conclusion. In Hitchcock's *Notorious,* Grant was perfectly beastly to Ingrid Bergman, who adored him, but eventually he came to his senses.

Calling his "the longest romantic reign in the short history of the movies," Kael wrote of Cary Grant that "being the pursued doesn't make him seem weak or passively soft. It makes him glamorous and—since he is not as available as other men—far more desirable." Men identified with him, despite the glamour, because he epitomized "the subtle fantasy of worldly grace, of being so gallant and gentlemanly that every woman longs to be your date. And at that deluxe level, men want to be Cary Grant. Men as far apart as John F. Kennedy and Lucky Luciano thought that he should star in their life story."

He was a real actor, not only a star, and even if the Motion Picture Academy failed miserably to recognize that (during the forties Grant was noted for making films in which the other people got the Oscars), his fellow actors praised his craftmanship. Part of that was sheer physical agility, something he learned in the earliest phases of his career as an acrobat and vaudevillian. He made even speech balletic, giving lines his own trademark dash; impersonators over the years mocked him with a sing-songy "Judy-Judy-Judy" (something he said he never uttered in a film) and by jumping about the stage as if dodging bullets. Cary Grant made words dance and is best remembered in motion:

In *North by Northwest*, as Madison Avenue's Roger O. Thornhill, he races toward a cornfield in his drab but nattily tailored gray flannel suit ("a perfect forty-four long," a Georgetown tailor once said of Grant) to escape the attack of a crop-dusting plane that is dusting where there ain't no crops.

In *Holiday*, he does cartwheels and somersaults and plays defiant children's games with Katharine Hepburn, another great brat of the screen, both of them demonstrating their rejection of prepatterned lives that her fuddy-duddy parents have planned for them.

In *Gunga Din*, in addition to all the other derring-do, he waves and shouts frantically to persuade a huge elephant named Annie not to venture out onto the footbridge on which he and the title character not-so-gently sway in the wind.

In *Bringing Up Baby*, he doggedly chases a fox terrier named George all around a Connecticut estate because George is believed to have buried the precious missing bone of a dinosaur waiting for completion in a New York museum.

In *The Philadelphia Story,* having been thrown out of the house by Hepburn as the first act of a divorce, and having seen his golf clubs tossed after him like rubbish, he stalks back to the front door, grabs Hepburn's entire face in his hand, and shoves her back inside the house. In an interview, Grant said he may have been a little rough on Hepburn because she'd given him such a sound slapping in their big flop *Sylvia Scarlett* five years earlier.

Though he sang in only a couple films (*Suzy* and one he hated, *Night and Day,* a scrubbed-up Cole Porter story), there was something musical in almost all his performances. Michael Curtiz, tireless house director at Warner Bros., once said, "Some actors squeeze a line to death. Cary tickles it to life." He was asked to play the part of Henry Higgins in the film version of *My Fair Lady.* He declined.

Indeed, in his later years, he declined not only roles but awards. He wouldn't accept the American Film Institute's Life Achievement Award because doing so meant he would have to give a speech; Cary Grant was shy. AFI founder and producer George Stevens, Jr., whose father directed Grant in three films, said, "In person, he was every bit as suave and engaging and companionable as he appeared on the screen. He was really great fun to be with. He loved to tell stories. His background was from the circus and having been a straight man in vaudeville, so he was a real student of comedy. He loved to laugh."

Grant had such vitality on and off the screen that stories had him living the life of a devoted health nut. It was an image he tried to put to rest in an interview with Cleveland Amory a year before his death. "I must have read a hundred times about how I'm an exercise fanatic and I'm always on a strict diet and keep to a stern health regimen and spend hours doing yoga," he said. "And I don't do any of those things! I rarely exercise, I eat anything and everything, and the only thing I know about yoga is what I learned when I used to watch Barbara Hutton doing it, and that was forty years ago."

Barbara Hutton was one of his five wives. Yes, Cary Grant had five wives; how could he be that glamorous and not? Among the tantalizing tales about Grant was that he experimented with LSD during the sixties and his marriage to Dyan Cannon, but he said later that it was under a doctor's supervision (not the marriage, the drug) and was to have been therapeutic instead of recreational.

He was full of surprises right along, but the surprises never really threatened the image we treasured; nor do lingering rumors about an allegedly more-than-colorful sex life. For all the glitz and the dapper charm, he could summon up real power on the screen, too, and his first unrequited Oscar nomination was for a weepie called *None but the Lonely Heart*. The public didn't flock to that one, but it did to the three-hanky romance *An Affair to Remember* with Deborah Kerr in 1957. Grant used to say it was his most frequently requested film.

It's the movie in which he plays a rich playboy who has a serious shipboard romance with Kerr. Both plan to shed other entanglements and meet at the top of the Empire State Building. Why there? Because, Kerr says in the film, it's "the closest thing to heaven."

Cary Grant left the movies in part to spare us the pain of seeing him grow old on the screen, but he remained buoyant and youthful-acting in most of his public appearances.

A famous and apparently apocryphal telegram once sent him asked, HOW OLD CARY GRANT? The evasive reply allegedly came back, OLD CARY GRANT FINE. HOW YOU? Watching his movies now, seeing him bob and weave and dart about—nimble and frisky and laughing inside, at the crazy business of make-believe and maybe at his own irrepressible glamorousness—he is alive again, and all of us young with him.

Old Cary Grant fine. How you?

TOM SHALES, syndicated television critic of *The Washington Post*, won the Pulitzer Prize for Criticism in 1988. The same year, the American Society of Newspaper Editors gave him its award for distinguished newspaper writing, citing his appreciations of entertainment celebrities written upon their deaths. Shales's first job as a writer was at WRMN, a radio station in Elgin, Illinois, where he was born and grew up. He has reviewed movies for "Morning Edition" on National Public Radio and written for *Esquire*, *Life*, *Interview* and *Video Review*. He refuses to say how old he is, and his mother has agreed to say "no comment" when asked for the date of his birth. If he had his way, he would stay home all day and watch old movies on TV.